THE

WORLD SITUATION

AND

God's Move

⑥

WITNESS LEE

Living Stream Ministry
Anaheim, California • www.lsm.org

First Edition, December 1982.

ISBN 978-0-87083-092-1

Published by

Living Stream Ministry
2431 W. La Palma Ave., Anaheim, CA 92801 U.S.A.
P. O. Box 2121, Anaheim, CA 92814 U.S.A.

Printed in the United States of America

16 17 18 19 20 21 / 13 12 11 10 9 8 7

CONTENTS

PREFACE

The events of world history have been sovereignly arranged by God for Him to carry out His purpose. As Acts 17:26 says, He "hath made of one blood all nations of men for to dwell on all the face of the earth, and hath determined the times before appointed, and the bounds of their habitation." The rise and fall of the kingdoms of earth and the boundaries of all the nations have been predetermined by Him.

In these messages, given in Anaheim, California in the spring of 1981, we have tried to present a view of world events from this perspective. Since the church comes out of mankind, we as His chosen ones need to have this view of man's history.

God's move among men is wrapped up with the course of history. Whether we speak of His becoming flesh through the incarnation, or of the spread of the gospel, or of the raising up of the church life, or of the preparation of the bride, all these aspects of His move require the proper environment, as far as the world situation is concerned.

We trust that these messages will make the reader more aware of God's arrangement of world affairs, more concerned about the crucial time in which we live, and more burdened for His ultimate move in what might be the ultimate world situation.

Witness Lee

Anaheim, California
September 1982

Chapter One

THE WORLD SITUATION
IN RELATION TO GOD'S MOVE ON EARTH

(1)

Scripture Reading: Acts 17:24-27; Dan. 2:21; 4:17

Prayer: Lord Jesus, we love You. We like to tell You how much we love You. You are our God. You are very God and You are very Man. We love You because of this. In You we see God, we find God, and we obtain God. In You we also see man, a proper man. We worship You that today You are on the throne. How we worship You! We worship You as the exalted Man on the throne of God. How we thank You that today we are preaching You, declaring You, and ministering You to all the needy ones! Thank You, Lord Jesus. We exalt You in our meeting. You are God's exalted Head and also our Lord of lords. We give You all the glory. Thank You for Your redemption. Thank You for Your life. Thank You for all You are. In Your precious name we worship You. Amen.

OUT OF ONE BLOOD

The church comes out of mankind. To have the proper church life, we must therefore know the world situation. This situation is under God's sovereign arrangement. I like Acts 17:26: "And hath made of one blood all nations of men for to dwell on all the face of the earth, and hath determined the times before appointed, and the bounds of their habitation."

God made all the nations out of one blood. Regardless of all the different skin colors, God made all the races out of the blood He created in Adam. One blood means one person, that is, Adam. In a sense we should not have concepts about people because of their skin color; all of us are out of the same blood.

THE TIMES AND THE BOUNDARIES

God determined the appointed times and boundaries. The continent of America was discovered by Columbus, but it was not up to him. God ordained that this continent be occupied just by the Indians and that the rest of the world be kept in ignorance of it until about five hundred years ago. What was it that inspired Columbus to sail west? Could he have had a dream? When I was in school, I learned the poem about Columbus, called "Sail On." The sailors were angry at such a seemingly endless voyage with no sight of land and wanted to turn back. Columbus kept telling them, "Sail on!" There were great men in the past. Solomon was the wisest of men. No one before Columbus, though, had the inspiration to reach the eastern lands by sailing west.

The time was before appointed. God made the appointment when America should be exposed to the descendants of Japheth. You remember Noah's prophecy: "God shall enlarge Japheth..." (Gen. 9:27). Now the time was ripe for Japheth to be enlarged and to spread abroad. The example of the discovery of America is only one illustration of how the spreading of the nations, their boundaries, and their time are all determined by God's appointment.

Since God made man in His image and made all peoples out of one blood, He surely took an interest in the territories the various nations would occupy and the seasons when they would be in the ascendancy. Where the bears, lions, and tigers would be was not of much concern to Him; but man, made in His image and therefore like Him (like a photograph of Him) surely has had his seasons and boundaries appointed by God (see Dan. 2:21; 4:17).

GOD'S ACCOMPLISHMENTS

After Adam took in the evil one and had his eyes opened to see, not the good things but his nakedness, God came and called him, "Adam, where art thou?" (Gen. 3:9). Adam was hiding himself in shame and fear. He had covered himself with the dying fig leaves. God, of course, said He would discipline him, but He also gave him the promise that the seed of the woman would bruise the serpent's head (v. 15). This was the way the serpent would be destroyed.

Four thousand years went by. Mankind meantime went further and further downhill. They went down to idolatrous Babel, trying to erect a tower to spread abroad their own name. This caused God to call out one man, Abraham, and to promise him that He would bless the whole earth through him (Gen. 22:18). This promise, made midway in the four thousand years, was stronger and more definite than the one to Adam. Still mankind had to wait for the fulfillment.

Finally the Lord Jesus came. God came! This time it was not in the form of a man, as in the case of His visit with Abraham (Gen. 18). Now He came by way of pregnancy. He came by way of getting into man's blood, man's flesh. He stayed in a virgin's womb for nine months and then came forth as an ordinary baby. He was born, not in a hospital nor even in an inn, for there was no room for Him there; He was placed in a manger. Thus God put on human nature.

Then He lived a human life for thirty-three and a half years. He was not in a rich family, nor did He have an easy life. At the end He was put to death by crucifixion. He was buried, and He arose.

Why did He take this path? All He went through was to accomplish one goal: to bring God into man by redemption and resurrection.

THE RIGHT SITUATION

For Redemption

For these great things to be accomplished, there had to be the right situation. Take the matter of the crucifixion as an example. In the Old Testament there was the prophecy which hinted that the Lord Jesus would hang on a tree (Deut. 21:22-23; Gal. 3:13). In typology, there was the brass serpent which was lifted up on a pole (Num. 21:8-9; John 3:14). The Roman Empire used crucifixion to carry out the death penalty for the lowest class of criminals and for slaves who were guilty of rebellion. By using this means to put to death the Lord Jesus, the Roman Empire was the instrument for the prophecies regarding Christ's death to be fulfilled.

For Christ's great accomplishments to be carried out, there was the need for the Roman Empire to be established. After I was saved I was interested in studying world history and comparing it with the Bible so that I might know more concerning the spiritual things. I learned the significance of many things from reading and studying world history. The rise of nations began after Babel. The Jews, because they offended God, lost their homeland about 600 B.C. when Nebuchadnezzar destroyed Jerusalem and carried many of them captive to Babylon. Not too long after, the supremacy of Babylon passed to Media-Persia. Persia is the present Iran. The Medo-Persian Empire controlled the lands formerly under Babylon, including the land of Israel. Then a little over 300 years B.C. Alexander the Great of Macedonia defeated Media-Persia and ruled those lands. He was only about thirty when he died.

Following the death of Alexander, his kingdom broke up. In the interval before the rise of the Roman Empire, there was no world empire controlling the nations around the Mediterranean. Wars and disturbances were common. Gradually the Romans, especially under Julius Caesar, defeated all the surrounding nations. Octavian, Julius Caesar's grandnephew, defeated Egypt. With this conquest all the lands around the Mediterranean were brought under Roman control. Octavian was the adopted heir of Julius Caesar. In 27 B.C. Octavian took the title Augustus and became the first emperor.

It was during the reign of Augustus that Christ was born. Luke 2:1 says, "And it came to pass in those days, that there went out a decree from Caesar Augustus, that all the world should be taxed." The Lord Jesus was born under the rule of the first formal Caesar of the Roman Empire. It was God's ordination that the Roman Empire should be in control of the Mediterranean area during the time of Christ.

The order which Rome brought to that warring region made it possible for the Lord Jesus to be born peacefully into mankind. The Roman method of capital punishment, crucifixion, made possible the fulfillment of the prophecies concerning His death.

For the Spread of the Gospel

The spread of the gospel after the resurrection and ascension of Christ was greatly facilitated by the common language, the single rule, the roads, and the domestic order that Rome established.

Greek was the language of the educated classes. The New Testament, though written almost entirely by Jews—Luke was the only exception—was written in Greek, not Hebrew. Even before the rise of the Roman Empire, about three centuries before Christ, the Hebrew Old Testament was translated into Greek. This version, called the Septuagint, was translated by seventy scholars in Alexandria, Egypt. When the Lord Jesus was on earth, many times the Scriptures He quoted were from the Septuagint.

Rome called its conquered lands provinces, for example, Galatia, Asia, Achaia, and Macedonia. With all these provinces being united under Rome, people were free to cross borders without restrictions. Such a situation was a great convenience to those who traveled to spread the gospel. In addition, ships were available for crossing the Mediterranean; for traveling by land the roads the Romans built crossed the whole empire.

The peace and order that prevailed further encouraged travel, thus aiding the spread of the gospel. Robbery was kept under control. It was reasonably safe to travel without fear of being robbed or killed. Roman citizens were under the full protection of the law. Paul himself claimed this right. When he was about to be scourged, he protested to the centurion, "Is it lawful for you to scourge a man that is a Roman, and uncondemned?" (Acts 22:25). The chief captain was afraid "after he knew that he was a Roman, and because he had bound him" (v. 29). Later when the Jews, his own countrymen, were accusing him before Festus, he claimed his right as a Roman citizen and appealed to Caesar (Acts 25:11). Thus he was protected.

The Roman Empire, then, was appointed by God to provide

the situation in which redemption could be accomplished and the gospel spread.

SATAN'S COUNTERMOVE

Satan followed. What God uses, Satan also comes along to use in order to cause damage. The emperors began to persecute the Christians, and countless numbers were martyred. Persecution, as we know, did not terminate the Christians; it rather helped them. Then Satan changed his strategy. Under the rule of Constantine the Great the Roman Empire made Christianity legal, and Christians had the full freedom of worship. Because of the favors he granted the Christians, thousands of pagans were baptized and became Christians in name. These were the tares spoken of in Matthew 13:24-30. That ruined Christianity.

Constantine was a clever politician. He wanted to bring all the warring factions of the empire together. Realizing that Christianity could be a peaceful influence, he decided that first the conflicts that were raging among theologians must be resolved. He therefore convened a council to meet at Nicaea to discuss the matters of Christology and the Trinity. These were the two main issues that were being fought over, even as they are today. Constantine himself presided over the council. Under his influence the Nicene Creed was drawn up (A.D. 325). He acted openly as head of the Church, which in his reign was first called Catholic; at the same time he kept his title of high priest of the heathen.

This ruin progressed from the fourth to the sixth centuries, by which time the papal system was fully established. With this the Roman Catholic Church reached its full development; it claimed to be the one, universal church (catholic means universal) and exercised worldly power over people and nations. No protest or dissent was tolerated. Over the centuries when it held sway, the Roman Catholic Church killed more genuine Christians than the pagan Roman Empire had killed. Under such a dark Church, the so-called Dark Ages were produced, lasting about ten centuries, from about A.D. 500 to 1500.

THE REFORMATION

Around 1500 the Reformation came in. God used Germany to protect Martin Luther. But once again, what God used Satan also used. Luther was bold in defending justification by faith. When it came to the matter of the church, however, he was weak. Satan used Germany to interfere with Luther's ministry. The first state church was formed in Germany; this was due to Luther's weakness. Even today this state church exists in Germany, supported by public taxes.

Other state churches sprang up. There are the state churches of Denmark, Norway, and Sweden. The monarchs of these countries are the heads of the state church. The same is true of Great Britain; Queen Elizabeth is the head of the Anglican Church. What a ruin to the church of God, which is the Body of Christ!

This historical background shows how God used the world situation in the carrying out of His economy and then how Satan followed, using the same means, to ruin God's work.

Around the time of the Reformation, another thing happened: the discovery of the new land by Columbus. These two things, the Reformation and the discovery of the new land, liberated human mentality. Science and scientific knowledge grew, leading to modern machines and weapons. The free mentality plus the newly discovered land changed the world a lot.

This was the period of time when Spain was the dominant power. It was Spain which provided the support for Columbus' voyages. This gave Spain the right to lay claim to vast portions of the Americas. Even today in the southwest of the United States the Spanish influence is apparent. Many cities along the West Coast, like Los Angeles and San Francisco, have Spanish names. Spain reached out even to the Far East and took possession of the Philippines. As a result, the Catholic influence there is still strong. All of Central and South America, except Brazil, speak Spanish because of the Spanish conquests.

Until the close of the sixteenth century, Spain was the leading power on earth. If she had remained on top, the whole world would be under Catholicism, as is the case with Latin America. God could not allow this. Therefore He raised up the small island of Britain, and in 1588 the British navy dealt a fatal blow to Spain's supremacy by defeating the larger, seemingly better equipped, Spanish Armada.

THE DEVELOPMENT OF THE CHURCH LIFE

With the coming of the Reformation the Bible was released. This, coupled with the free thinking that developed once Catholicism's hold on the mind was broken, led Christians to the discovery of many new truths in the Bible. It seemed that everyone who discovered a new truth became the founder of a new denomination. There were a number of Brethren churches which began during this period of the seventeenth and eighteenth centuries. The Grace Brethren and the Mennonites were two of them. All these newly formed denominations were persecuted by both the Catholic Church and the state churches. This was true of the state churches even in northern Europe. These freethinking Christians were thus in peril for their lives.

The Moravian Brethren

At this very time God raised up Count Zinzendorf, a wealthy German who owned a large estate in Saxony. He invited the persecuted Christians to come and stay there. From many places they came, but mostly from Moravia. With their varied denominational backgrounds, they were soon quarreling about the presbytery, baptism, and other doctrines. Finally, Zinzendorf called the leaders together. He reminded them how they had come together as brothers to escape persecution. They must stop their dissenting ways, he said, and sign a contract to cease arguing and simply be one in Christ. This they agreed to do. After that they had the Lord's table. There was a great outpouring of the Holy Spirit. Eventually, hundreds of the so-called Moravian Brethren went out to other lands, especially to the newly found land of America. Even today there are a number of Moravian Churches in the United States.

On one of these ships bound for America was John Wesley. A great storm arose, causing the passengers to fear for their lives. Wesley, a revivalist but not sure of his salvation, noticed a group of passengers praying together. As a result of his contact with these Moravian Brethren, Wesley eventually came into assurance of salvation. After a time in America, he returned to England and then went on to Saxony to spend time with the Moravians. Had he not been burdened for England, he would have liked to remain with them. This was the time of the French Revolution. Those revolutionary ideas were gaining ground in England, and there was fear that the government itself might be overthrown. It was through the preaching of John Wesley and George Whitefield, those powerful open-air evangelists, that the gospel prevailed over the revolutionary tendencies and England was spared. British society was changed as a result of their work.

The practice of the church life by those with Count Zinzendorf marked a beginning. It was good, but it was not adequate. Their light was limited, but we consider that theirs was the first practice of the church life in the Lord's recovery after the Reformation.

The Brethren

About a century later, in the 1820s, God raised up the Brethren in England, under the leadership of John Nelson Darby. Oh, the light that flooded in! Luther had unlocked the Bible from prison, but it remained for Darby and his contemporaries to open it. Even today the best theological seminaries follow the Brethren teaching. Yet, they would not take the Brethren way in the matter of the church life.

The Brethren movement, according to an article by D. M. Panton, was stronger and more prevailing than the Reformation under Luther. To the world, however, it was unknown. This was because the early Brethren would have nothing to do with the worldly ways the Reformation had followed. Martin Luther gained the support of princes and other worldly rulers to advance the cause of the Reformation. Newspapers were printed for the first time in the 1500s; these were used to spread propaganda for the Reformation. The Brethren had no publicity; everything about them was kept covered. It is hard to find a photograph, for example, of J. N. Darby. They did not have biographies nor autobiographies. A number among them who were lords and ladies renounced their titles.

When Jamaica in the British West Indies suffered a ruinous storm during the last century, the British Brethren assemblies sent aid to the believers there. The amount they sent greatly surpassed what the British government provided.

THE RISE OF BRITAIN

There was still the need for the gospel to be spread to Africa and to Asia. There was also the need for the spread of the light seen by the Brethren to every part of the earth. How was this spreading to come about?

After the defeat of the Spanish Armada, Spain's power declined while that of Britain rose. Gradually she became an empire, with colonies all around the earth. It was called the empire without a sunset. For more than two centuries the colonies were farms, providing her with the goods she needed and making her wealthy.

During the days of Britain's preeminence, the Protestant influence reached to every continent. Most missionaries in the past were British. The money used for the spread of the gospel was largely in pounds sterling, not United States dollars. It was in England that many spiritual giants were raised up. Great teachers among the Brethren wrote hundreds of books for the release of the truth. Light was released by the speakers at the Keswick Convention.

Now, however, especially since World War II, Great Britain has lost her colonies, the source of her wealth. Instead of her islands being gardens, they have had to become farms. Britain was not faithful to God or to man. In World War I she promised the Jews to make Palestine their homeland if they would help in the fight against Germany. At the same time she secretly promised the Jordanians, who were Arabs, that Palestine would become theirs if they would join in fighting against the Turks. When the war was over, the Jews and Jordanians were both offended at this duplicity.

THE UNITED STATES AS A WORLD POWER

The United States followed Britain as a world power.

Before the discovery of America, the connecting center for the whole world was the Holy Land. Though it is located in the western part of Asia, it joins Asia, Europe, and Africa. God sovereignly made the Holy Land the focus of the ancient populated world, so that the gospel could be formed and spread from there.

Since World War II, the United States has been the heart of the populated world. Its climate is temperate. It lies between two great oceans, which are like the wings of an eagle.

Whatever the United States does, the entire world follows. This is true financially, industrially, scientifically, politically, militarily, religiously, scripturally, and spiritually! Even in language, it is American English, not British, which prevails.

Why has God ordained this? It is for His move on earth to carry out His recovery. The Roman Empire was for the gospel. Germany was for the Reformation. Britain was for the spreading of the gospel and of the truth. Now the United States has become the center for the recovery. From here it can spread to all the continents in a world-wide language. Wherever we are from, we must appreciate America. God will use America to spread His recovery so that the Lord may return.

THE WORLD SITUATION
IN RELATION TO GOD'S MOVE ON EARTH

(2)

Scripture Reading: Acts 17:26-27; 1:8

THE PRESERVATION OF AMERICA

Around 1500 two important events occurred. One was the Reformation, which opened the gate of the prison of Catholicism and thus released the human mentality to search for the truth. The other was the discovery of the Americas, two vast continents which until that time were virtually unknown and uninhabited.

When God created the earth, the continent of North America was included not by chance. Under God's sovereignty it remained hidden for many centuries, preserved for God's purpose. If you study a world globe, you will readily see how vital this land mass is to mankind. It lies between two oceans. The Atlantic and Pacific are like two wings of an eagle, which is the symbol of America. In the early days of American independence the eagle was chosen as the emblem of the new nation. Without its two wings, an eagle is powerless. The United States derives much of its strength from the two oceans on its shores.

The whole world today looks to the United States. The American dollar is universally desired. The dollar is one of the standards by which other currencies are measured. This is so, even though the United States is still a young country, less than three hundred years old. Other nations, like Israel, look to America for financial aid. Another indication of the

United States being the world's focus is the air traffic it has with other nations. To fly from the West Coast to the Far East does not cost much more than to fly from Los Angeles to New York. How can the price be that little? It is because of the great abundance of traffic. Many different airlines fly these routes daily.

God preserved America for fifty-five hundred years. He allowed the fallen descendants of Adam to ruin all the other continents, but the Americas He kept undamaged. Parking spaces are reserved for VIPs; we should consider that all Americans are VIPs. The land of America has been reserved for them!

We all need a grateful attitude toward God for preserving America. Though I am Chinese by birth, I do appreciate the United States. It is the top country in the world. God has watched over it.

THE SPREAD OF THE EUROPEANS

With the release of the human mentality around the time of the Reformation, new, aggressive ideas came in. Europeans wanted to explore distant places. There was much competition among them. Spain took the lead to send out explorers. Thus, many of the new territories came into her hand. Throughout South America, Central America, and the southwestern part of the United States the Spanish influence is still apparent. Spanish names like San Jose and Mission Viejo, with the letter j pronounced like an h, are examples of this. Spain's preeminence on the seas ended with the defeat of the Spanish Armada by the smaller British fleet in 1588. This defeat restricted the further spread of Catholicism by Spain.

THE RISE OF CAPITALISM

The new ideas of the sixteenth century led to modern science and the development of machines. The wealthy could set up factories which turned out goods much more quickly than had been possible before. The laborers worked hard for little pay. In effect, the wealthy owners were robbing the poor working class and pocketing their money. These were the millionaire capitalists. How was this problem of balancing the wealth to be solved?

The government favored the ever-expanding output of the factories because it meant more taxes, that is, increased revenue for the government. Thus, the factories got bigger and bigger, until eventually overproduction resulted. With goods not being sold, many of the factories then had to close down, causing unemployment and economic hardship. Where were markets to be found for these manufactured goods?

IMPERIALISM

The rich countries looked overseas for new markets. They built up their navies and armies and went to the backward countries of Asia and Africa to subdue them. With a small number of men they would come into a country in their gunboats and force that country to sign a treaty promising to provide a market for their goods. This is imperialism. For my college graduation in 1926 this is the topic I chose to write on for my thesis.

THE FADING OF BRITAIN

I love Britain, but how pitiful she is today! She has been stripped of almost everything. She has lost most of Ireland. Her islands, which formerly were beautiful gardens, have had to become farms to feed her people. Her colonies around the globe without sunset, which were the farms supplying her people with abundance, are gone. Spiritually speaking, too, she has become poverty-stricken. Last century scores of spiritual books—weighty, enlightening, life-imparting—appeared. What book of spiritual weight has come forth from her in recent years?

God did use Britain. She was raised up for advancing God's purpose. She was His instrument to put down the previous world power, Catholic Spain. However, she was proud, mistreating weaker peoples. All men are made in God's image, regardless of their skin color. In the early days of the church, five prophets and teachers are mentioned in Antioch. One of these, Niger, was a black, judging from his name (Acts 13:1). It offends God when people are despised because of their skin color. Pride was a problem with the spiritual ones in Britain too. I believe that pride has been a factor in the fading of Britain.

THE DECLINE OF CHRISTIANITY

As for the church, the Brethren were much used by God to bless the church with the knowledge of the Bible. But, Satan came in to use this very knowledge to ruin the assemblies. What God uses to bless, Satan uses to ruin. The Brethren were divided into at least a thousand different sects by this matter of doctrine. They split hairs not mainly over matters of truth, but over fine doctrinal points. We must be on the alert to profit from their failure. This is why I do not like to talk to you about doctrines. If we have doctrinal debates, we are sectarian already.

In the last century and the beginning of this one many spiritual books containing new light came out in English. Besides the great teachers among the Brethren, there were evangelists like C. H. Spurgeon, Charles Finney, D. L. Moody, and R. A. Torrey who were outside the Brethren. There were teachers like Andrew Murray, Mrs. Penn-Lewis, A. B. Simpson, T. Austin-Sparks, G. Campbell Morgan, and the Keswick speakers. W. H. Griffith Thomas and Frederick Lewis Godet were two of the expositors. All this spiritual output has largely ceased. Who today is a man of God with some spiritual weight? In the twenty years that I have been in this country, from what I have observed, not one book of spiritual significance has been published.

THE KERNEL OF THE BIBLE NEGLECTED

If you read church history and the biographies of spiritual men of the past, you will see that three things have been accomplished. The gospel is being preached, the Bible is being taught for the edification of the saints, and the scriptural way of meeting is being practiced. Even though there is much confusion and mixture throughout Christianity, these things at least are known and followed in some measure. However, the very kernel of the Bible, the focus of God's economy, has been neglected throughout the centuries.

The Bible teaching of the Brethren is the best, and they meet according to the Bible. And Brother Nee's book, *The Normal Christian Church Life,* makes the matter of how to meet even clearer than the Brethren teachings. The Brethren preach the gospel, as do the other evangelicals. These three things are not sufficient, however. The Apostle Paul's completing ministry is missing. There is the need to have Christ as our life, as the real contents of the church. The reality of the church is more than a meeting of the saints. It is not merely a collection of seeking saints. It is Christ realized, experienced, enjoyed, lived out, and expressed. A people in this experience are the reality of the Body of Christ. They are a golden lampstand.

THE RECOVERY OF THE CENTRAL VISION

The Lord used the Roman Empire to form and spread the gospel. He used Germany to support the Reformation. He used Great Britain for the preaching of the gospel and the spreading of the truth to the uttermost part of the earth. There is still one matter which the Lord has not worked out. According to my understanding, the Lord has preserved one part of the globe, the United States, for this very thing to be accomplished.

On the American continent over two hundred years ago the Lord used a group of men to form a country democratic and constitutional, where people would have the full freedom to speak what they believe. Do you not believe that the Lord has sovereignly raised up and preserved this country where we can speak so freely what we see from the Bible? As long as we are law-abiding citizens, this freedom is ours. Hallelujah for such a country!

Surely the position and condition of the United States are not an accident. Acts 17:26 says that God "determined the times before appointed, the bounds of their habitation." The time was appointed by our God; the boundaries were drawn by Him. As He prepared the Roman Empire, Germany, and Great Britain in times gone by, so He has prepared the United States. For what purpose? It was not merely for the preaching of the gospel, the teaching of the truth, and

the scriptural way of meeting. These things have been practiced for centuries. Yes, we must continue these practices. We
must preach the gospel adequately. We must teach the Bible
and seek to bring others to the full knowledge of the truth; for
this we need to respect and know God's Word. We must also
come together according to the Bible to have a proper church
life.

These three things, however, are not sufficient. We must be
for the central vision of God's economy. We must live Christ,
be filled with Him, and have Him as our daily living and as
the practical, actual contents of the church life that we may be
His living Body to express Him. Then every local church will
be a golden lampstand, and the bride will be prepared for the
Bridegroom.

THE WORLD SITUATION
IN RELATION TO GOD'S MOVE ON EARTH

(3)

Scripture Reading: Acts 17:24-27; Dan. 2:21; 4:17

For God to carry out His purpose, He has arranged the world situation. History is meaningful when we realize this. Just a few years before Christ was born, the Roman Empire became fully established. Everything was ready for Christ to be born according to the prophecies in the Old Testament. Why, for example, did Mary have to go to Bethlehem? She was in Galilee, but Augustus issued a decree that required her to go to Bethlehem. If Christ had been born in Nazareth, where Mary was living, it would have been contrary to the prophecy (Micah 5:2). The Roman Empire also provided a way for the gospel to be spread.

Later, Germany was used by God to support the Reformation, and Great Britain in more recent times was raised up by God to further carry out His purpose. After defeating the Spanish Armada in 1588, she became the leading world power. Through her the gospel was spread throughout the world. Because of her unfaithfulness and pride, however, she has lost her preeminence.

Britain's unfairness was demonstrated when the League of Nations was in effect. The League had been formed after World War I under the direction of President Woodrow Wilson, though the United States did not join. Britain, France, Japan, and China all belonged, along with many other nations. Britain and France were in favor of the League of Nations as the means to keep Germany under restraint. The other nations wanted to be protected. In 1931 Japan invaded Manchuria, which was part of China. When China appealed to the League of Nations, the League sent a mission to Manchuria under the chairmanship of the British Lord Lytton to investigate. However, the League of Nations was not able to do anything to correct the situation.

JAPAN

This weakness in dealing with Japanese aggression emboldened Japan to invade northern China in 1937. The United States had previously realized the need for a strong China to maintain the balance of power on the other side of the Pacific. Thus, under the United States' leadership, a treaty had been drawn up in 1921 and 1922, respecting the independence and territorial integrity of China and promising to maintain an Open Door there. Japan was one of the signatories to this Nine-Power Treaty. When Japan invaded China, Roosevelt, who was President at the time, reminded Japan of its signature on this treaty and demanded that Japan withdraw. Japan refused. China again appealed to the League of Nations, which again proved unable to help.

In 1941 Japan sent a delegation to the United States to gain more favorable treatment for Japan. Negotiations were still going on when Japanese planes attacked Pearl Harbor. With the bombing of Pearl Harbor, the United States declared war on Japan; there was only one vote against it in Congress. A few days later Congress also declared war on Germany and Italy. The Chinese were joyful that after four years of trying to resist Japan, they were finally being joined by the United States. With the aid of its top-notch generals—Eisenhower in Europe, MacArthur in the Far East, and Marshall as Chief of Staff—the war was won.

RUSSIA

Russia in territory and population was the largest country in Europe. While the other European nations were striving to gain world markets for their goods, however, Russia was still backward. Their ways were Oriental, not Western. During the reign of Peter the Great, Russia became a great power. It adopted western ways and gained access to the sea. The Bible speaks of Russia as Gog and Magog (see Ezek. 38; 39; Rev. 20) and says that this people will be rebellious against God till the end of the thousand years. The territory assigned to them is in the frozen north.

The czars tried again and again to gain a warm water outlet to the sea. They tried to get a port on the Black Sea so that they could go through the Aegean Sea, between Greece and Turkey, into the Mediterranean and out through Gibraltar into the Atlantic Ocean. Britain prevented this by persuading the Turks to watch over the Aegean and by using Malta and Gibraltar to guard the Mediterranean. When the Suez Canal was built in Egypt, the British also controlled this, again preventing the Russians from gaining an outlet to the sea. The czars then tried to get through the Persian Gulf into the Indian Ocean, but once again the British thwarted their efforts by influencing Persia.

Still with the aim of getting a warm water port, the czars had begun work in 1891 on the Trans-Siberian railroad. It began operating in 1901, though the last section was not completed till 1916. It extended from Moscow to Vladivostok on the Sea of Japan, was some five thousand miles in length, and cost millions of dollars to build. The czars were also able to gain eastern Siberia from China because the foolish emperor considered such a frozen land was not worth keeping. The Siberian railroad extended through this area also. Then the czars again got the emperor to agree to allow Russia to build the Chinese Eastern Railway across Manchuria and partially to control the province. In 1898 Russia leased the Liaotung Peninsula from China; the railroad was extended into that area. At the tip of the peninsula the Russians built the commercial port of Dairen and the naval base of Port Arthur. This meant the Russian navy had ships at Port Arthur. This was just across the sea from my home town of Chefoo.

When Britain saw that Russia had gained ports in the Far East, she influenced Japan to fight Russia. This agreed with Japanese interests, since Japan wanted the areas of China that Russia was controlling. Japan made an alliance with Great Britain in 1902, and war broke out in 1904. Japan defeated Russia and thus gained control of Korea. Russian troops had to withdraw from Manchuria. Japan was given Port Arthur and Dairen and took over the Russian rights in Manchuria.

The Japanese presence on the mainland led in 1931 to its invasion of Manchuria and eventually to the war in the Pacific. In 1932 the United States under President Hoover and Secretary of State Stimson declared it would not recognize Japan's territorial gains in Manchuria. In 1937 President Roosevelt also condemned Japanese aggression against China. In the fall of 1943 Roosevelt, Churchill, and Chiang Kai-shek met at Cairo for a conference to discuss the war and the postwar problems. When Roosevelt proposed getting rid of the Japanese emperor, Chiang Kai-shek advised against this, pointing out that the emperor was needed as a figurehead in order to keep the Japanese people under control. At the secret Yalta agreements in 1945 Roosevelt agreed to give Stalin Russia's former rights in Manchuria, which Japan had taken over. These agreements were made without China's knowledge.

Two months after the Yalta agreements, Roosevelt died. When Truman came into the Presidency, he was deeply concerned about bringing an end to the war. To hasten the end, he gave instructions that the atomic bomb be dropped on Japan. The emperor wanted to surrender immediately, but the generals held off. After the second bomb was dropped, the emperor unconditionally surrendered. On August 8, two days before Japan's offer became public, Russia declared war on Japan and sent its army into Manchuria, not to defeat the Japanese but to take the surrender. Gradually with the help of Russia, China became a Communist country. The United States withdrew.

The two Communist countries, Russia and China, should have been friendly toward each other, but six or seven years after the Communist takeover of China they had a dispute over the territory of Siberia. This led to a break and an end to their friendship. This was the Lord's sovereignty! If these two big Communist countries became one, it would be a menace to the entire world.

To be a significant power in the world today a nation must

have a big territory and a big population. This is demonstrated by Japan's attempt to take over China. Japan was a real power, with a navy, air force, and army. Even before they invaded, their learned ones warned them that it would be an impossible task. Japan was like a small snake; it could not swallow such a big prey! If they attempted it, their stomach would burst and they would die. Their statesmen urged them to be friendly toward China, rather than attack it. These wise words went unheeded. Japan first invaded North China, then Shanghai, then Nanking. In spite of all their forces, their bombings, their brutality toward the women, they were utterly unable to subdue so many millions of people.

Besides a large territory and a big population, natural resources and skills are also needed in order for a country to be powerful today. Only three nations have these four things: the United States, China, and Russia. Although China is backward in skills, it is making progress. Their nuclear science industry is developing. Their resources are rich, but underdeveloped. For this reason they need the United States. They need American money and skill to develop their iron, copper, silver, and coal mines. They need technology for working their oil fields.

The United States, Russia, and China are a strange triangle. Though two are Communist, they cannot work together. Russia is always opposed to the United States. In this three-angle struggle, Russia and the United States are competing. Who will gain the support of the third country? The United States will win China. The United States needs China to balance Russia; China needs the support of the United States to build the country.

Who can deal with this northern bear? Who can deal with Gog and Magog? God has been restricting this people who oppose Him. First He used Britain. Now He is using the present situation to restrict Russia.

THE MIDDLE EAST

The situation in the Middle East is also under God's sovereignty. Among the Arab countries which are against Israel, only two are significant. One is a military power, Egypt; the other is a financial power, Saudi Arabia. Egypt is favorable to the United States. Saudi Arabia, which has become wealthy because of its oil, is not favorable toward Israel, but it is friendly toward Egypt. The other Arab countries proved in the 1967 war that they lacked the strength to fight. Thus the Middle East situation is favorable for Israel.

Today we can see the fulfillment of God's promise to Abraham, Israel's forefather: "I will bless them that bless thee, and curse him that curseth thee" (Gen. 12:3). Russia is cursing Israel and is under God's curse. The United States is blessing Israel and is under God's blessing. The billions of dollars in financial aid that the United States has sent to Israel has brought God's blessing to the United States.

THE UNITED STATES

Today the world is under the leadership of the United States. God has preserved this country and blessed her with riches. He has sovereignly prepared her for the carrying out of the final stage of His recovery. Because there is freedom of speech, we are free to spread the light we have seen in the Word.

The situation of this country is also good for the practice of the church life. It is peaceful, comfortable, and prosperous. Unfortunately, this very situation also makes it easy for evil to flourish. American society can ruin the young people if they are not in the church life. To find a good job with good pay is fairly easy. After the eight hours of work a day, however, there is time, money, and opportunity to engage in many evil things. Not all Americans are bad, of course. Many are good; this can be seen when it is time to vote. But still the evil influence is there. In any case, the United States is the best place for us to meet together to have the church life.

The United States is also the center when it comes to travel. From any part of the world one can reach this country by plane within eighteen hours. Even far-off Australia and New Zealand are no farther away than this. The international airports like those in New York, Los Angeles, and Dallas are busy. The skies are full of planes transporting people to and from the United States.

American English is known by educated peoples world-wide. College graduates in any country can read the publications that come from the United States. Don't think that all these things happened accidentally. Don't forget Acts 17:26 which says that the times have been appointed by our God; the boundaries have been drawn by Him. He prepared the Roman Empire; He prepared Germany five hundred years ago; He prepared Great Britain. And today He has prepared the U.S.A., not just for the preaching of the gospel, nor just for the teaching of the truth, nor just for scriptural meetings, but for the preparation of the bride.

We must realize our tremendous responsibility with these four things. Firstly, we must preach the gospel properly, adequately, genuinely. Secondly, we must teach people the Bible, bringing them to the full knowledge of the truth. We must be a people who really respect and know God's divine Word. Thirdly, we must drop all kinds of religion and practices and come together according to the Bible. We have to be just genuine, biblical, bonafide, regenerated, saved, blood-washed Christians coming together to meet in the name of the Lord Jesus according to the Bible, with no organization.

However, although all these help, they still cannot satisfy God's desire. What is His desire? It is for us to live Christ, to have Christ as our living, to have Christ as the reality, the real contents of the church life, making every local church a golden lampstand. The Body life will reach the reality of Romans 12, and this will be the spontaneous preparation of the bride for His coming back. From the very beginning, even from eternity, this is what the Lord has desired. This is the goal of the Lord's recovery. This has been missed and neglected today, so it is toward this that the Lord is working.

The world situation has been prepared for this very purpose. The world situation under the leadership of the United States is fully for this purpose. America has been preserved for this. This is why God has blessed the United States with riches and influence. This is why so many people can easily come here.

There is one thing left for God to do. Many Christians have never seen the central vision of the Apostle Paul's completing ministry. Their Bible seemingly omits this part. In the Far East the Chinese Christians like Proverbs; they are Proverbs people, not Christ people. The Western Christians like Psalms; they are Psalms people. Instead of singing the Psalms, why would they not rather sing Ephesians 3: "...That He would grant you...to be strengthened with power through His Spirit into the inner man, that Christ may make His home in your hearts through faith...that you may be filled unto all the fullness of God" (vv. 16, 17, 19)? They prefer Psalm 23, about goodness and mercy following us. What is goodness? What is mercy? The real mercy is Christ's getting into us! The real goodness is Christ's having a home in us! We need to sing about Christ's making His home in us that eventually we may be filled unto all the fullness of God!

What hinders our singing about Christ's making His home in our hearts? Why wouldn't we sing that the church is the house of the living God? It is our background and atmosphere. What we are used to is: "Wives, submit yourselves unto your husbands....Husbands, love your wives....Love your neighbor as yourself...." We lack the environment to realize that we should live Christ. Christ Himself is our living, our love, our submission! He is the content of the church. The mystery of godliness is great: God was manifested in the flesh! We need to build up an atmosphere where these things are real to us.

The situation among Christians has been built up for nearly two thousand years until it has become like a pyramid full of garlic. So many are still living in this pyramid, so drugged that they do not recognize the garlic smell! They need to get out and into the fresh air! The fresh air is the Spirit, the Spirit that gives life, the life-giving Spirit. It is the indwelling Spirit, who is really the resurrected Christ, the One who died on the cross for us. This is the air we need to breathe! This is the Lord's recovery today.

The Lord is preparing the world situation. How grateful I am to the Lord that I am here! When I first came twenty-two years ago, I felt grieved to have lost my country. China was the great field of my work. There were hundreds of millions of people with one language. I could travel all over the country and speak to everyone. We had hundreds of churches. While Brother Nee was training people, I was the one who actually had charge of the entire work throughout the country. Then the political situation changed, and it was lost. Brother Nee told me and all the other co-workers that, no matter how I felt, I must leave the Mainland. When I asked why, he said I must go out, that one day the work there would be wiped out. If I went out, there would still be something left on the earth. At that time I was most sorrowful about our situation. Today I am grateful.

The whole world situation is under the Lord's sovereign maneuvering. Maneuvering is sometimes not a positive word, but it fits here. The Lord rules the world. He removes kings; He sets up kings (Dan. 2:21). He has restricted Russia. Even today He is restricting her, in spite of all her efforts to be the leading nation on earth. This is the age when the Lord will use the United States. If all these messages were given in the Chinese language, they would lie buried in that hard-to-understand language. As it is, they can be sent out all over the world as Life-studies, audio and video tapes, and books. With the word sent out in spoken and written form, I believe it will not be in vain. The Lord will follow His word to accomplish His purpose.

Brothers and sisters, open your eyes! Look at the entire globe, and get into the world situation. Look at the situation among Christians. Now you can understand the world situation in relation to His move. We should not be satisfied with only gospel preaching, Bible teaching, and scriptural meetings. We must be for the Apostle Paul's completing ministry, the central vision of God's economy. We must take Christ as our living. He must be the contents of the church life. Then He will gain His purpose. The churches will be golden lampstands, and the bride will be prepared.

It surely does not seem that there is time for God to raise up another country and take another step after this. I believe this is the last opportunity for God to prepare the bride. May we all see the seriousness of this time and realize our responsibility.

CHAPTER FOUR

GOD'S ULTIMATE MOVE
TO CARRY OUT HIS ETERNAL INTENTION

Scripture Reading: Matt. 28:18-19; Mark 16:15; Luke 24:47;
John 15:16a; Acts 1:8; Rev. 1:2, 12, 20; 19:7

What is God's ultimate move to carry out His intention?
God wants us to have Christ as life to us, flowing in us, saturating and permeating us, transforming us, conforming us,
and making us fit to be built up into His Body for His expression. Today, at the end of the twentieth century, this is what
our God is after. Here is where our focus also should be. Three
items have already been recovered: the preaching of the
gospel, the teaching of Bible truths, and the scriptural way of
meeting. Now this final matter must be our concern.

THE NEGLECT OF THE RECOVERED ITEMS

Scriptural Meetings

Of these three items, the third matter, that of meeting
together scripturally, has been lost among today's Christians.
What Christian group pays attention to this? The United
States is like an amphitheater, where all kinds of Christian
meetings can be seen. In some Christian groups there are
dramatic performances. They put on plays, with actors play-
ing the role of Peter or James, and they have rock music.
Other Christian groups meet in many different ways. There
are Pentecostal groups with dancing, jumping, or shouting.
Christians come together according to what suits their taste.
It seems little thought is given to meeting according to the
Bible. From around 1828 or 1829 the Brethren assemblies
were raised up and gradually began to make their meetings

very scriptural. But today even many of the Brethren assemblies have drifted away from having their meetings according to the Scriptures.

The Teaching of the Bible

Even the second matter that was recovered, the teaching of the Bible, has been neglected. Among the Closed Brethren, up to fifty years ago, there were good teachers of the Bible. Other Christians do not teach the Bible as much as they did. Many denominations simply have lectures or sermons with a Bible verse to support the speaker's point.

Gospel Preaching

If the scriptural way to meet and the sound teaching of the Bible have been neglected, what is left? Only gospel preaching. Yet much of today's preaching of the gospel is of the lowest standard. No doubt many of you have read the biographies of the great evangelists of the past. There were C. H. Spurgeon, D. L. Moody, Charles Finney, and George Whitefield. They used no gimmicks in their preaching. Their way was to pray. I read that once Charles Finney went into a factory and looked at the workers there. Just by his looking at them, a number of the workers wept and repented. What was the power behind these preachers? It was prayer. It was the spending of time in the Word of God, learning the Scriptures, and then selecting a subject from which to preach the gospel. This is the proper way.

Even those who play guitars in the meetings must be careful lest they offend the Lord. The Lord Jesus did not promise that if we play the guitar well, people would be saved. He said that we would be clothed with power from on high (Luke 24:49). The proper preaching comes from this power. Those who are concerned about the gospel need to fast and to pray desperately.

In Chefoo, beginning in 1940, the church spent the New Year's time in the preaching of the gospel. The New Year's celebrations in China are far more elaborate than Christmas here. Instead of buying food and making special dishes like everyone else, the saints made no special food preparations at all. The entire family, old and young, gave themselves to prayer. The whole church prayed. When the gospel was preached, there was an impact. In the marketplace and on the street the unbelievers warned their friends, "Don't go into that building. If you do, you will be subdued." The power was there. It came by prayer and by the Word. There was no special music, just some singing of choruses. It is a matter of prayer and the Word. The Apostles said, "We will give ourselves continually to prayer, and to the ministry of the word" (Acts 6:4).

Those who use rock music and other gimmicks in their gospel preaching may bring some people to the Lord by these means, but all such will be Moabites. They will be the sons of Lot, brought forth in an improper way, by Lot with his daughters (Gen. 19:30-38). Too many Christians are Moabites, born improperly. Today the Lord is again recovering the proper gospel preaching.

He is also recovering the proper teaching of the Bible. Last year an article was published in a Christian magazine saying that young people are attracted to the local churches because Witness Lee teaches the Bible. In most churches, the article said, the Bible is not taught. It also said that Witness Lee is a prolific writer and speaker. Yes, we have published one hundred twenty Life-studies on Genesis and already over one hundred on Exodus, which we have still not finished. In addition, there are Life-studies on Matthew, John, most of Paul's Epistles, and Revelation.

We must become familiar with the Bible. I hope all the young people would devour the Life-studies. If I had found such materials on the Bible when I was young, I would have stayed up late at night, swallowing up what was in them! But in those days very little was available. I bought nearly all the Christian books I could find, but they contained mostly husks, with very few grains. The Life-studies, though, are filled with nourishment on almost every line. If you love the Lord, you need to know the Bible. Twice the Bible tells us that the one who serves the Lord must be "apt to teach" (1 Tim. 3:2; 2 Tim. 2:24). Teach what? Not the newspaper! Not some magazine! No! He must be able to teach the Bible, book after book.

The Lord is also going to recover the proper way of meeting. How are we to determine if our way of meeting is scriptural? While no one can say that our meetings are unscriptural, it is hard to say what is the scriptural way to meet. We have published a book called *How to Meet*. If you read it, however, you will still be puzzled as to the proper way to meet. But I do know that dancing or rock music or drama in the meetings are wrong. Having soloists is wrong. These things are not only wrong, they are against the Lord's way. The Lord is still recovering the proper way to meet.

GOD'S FINAL MOVE

Suppose these three things are fully recovered. Are they God's ultimate move? Is gospel preaching God's ultimate move? Is teaching the Bible God's ultimate move? Is meeting according to the Bible God's ultimate move? What is God's ultimate move? It is to gain a people who have Christ as their life. We must live Him. We must not have just a doctrine, but a real life in our daily living. It must be our experience that Christ is the flowing life within us. As He saturates and permeates us, He supplies us with all His elements. Incarnation, humanity, human living, crucifixion, and resurrection—all these are carried out within us in this permeation. While His life is saturating us, it kills the negative things within us and supplies us with the divine element. We need to know this, not just in a doctrinal way, but as a reality in our experience. Then we need to know how to be transformed and how to grow into maturity. Furthermore, we must know by experience what it is to be built up, in order that Christ may have a Body.

God is not primarily after gospel preaching, nor Bible teaching, nor scriptural meetings. He wants Christ as the embodiment of God to become your life, and you as a member of Christ to become a part of His Body. Then Christ will have His Body. Then in every locality the Body will be expressed as a golden lampstand. This is the preparation of the bride.

Revelation 19:7 is yet to be fulfilled. It is when "His wife has made herself ready" that "the marriage of the Lamb is come."

Where among today's Christians is the bride being made ready? If you were to visit the different Christian meetings, you would realize how poor the situation is.

I am deeply burdened for you to see what God's ultimate move is. Do not think I have no earthly cares. I have a wife, children, grandchildren, daughters-in-law, and sons-in-law. Sometimes I have to see a doctor for a physical problem. Yes, I have my share of troubles; that is part of my lot as a human being. But none of these is my real concern. My real concern is how to present to the dear saints the Lord's ultimate move so that they may see it. I have a burden within. Where can the Lord get His heart's desire? Surely not in the idol temples, nor in the Moslem mosques, nor in the Catholic cathedrals. The Lord has no way. Even the proper gospel preaching, Bible teaching, and scriptural meetings have been neglected. Who cares about them? And who cares about God's ultimate move to carry out His eternal intention? Who even knows what God's eternal intention is?

When there is an evangelistic campaign today, the sponsors often depend on their organizational methods, rather than the power which comes through prayer and the Word. They advertise, they invite famous people to attend, and they ask the various denominations to band together to promote the campaign. In this way they are able to gather large crowds. Great numbers may respond. After a few years, however, what becomes of all these people? Consider all the campaigns that have been held these past thirty years. Where are those who were supposedly saved in them? On the one hand, I rejoice in the Lord. On the other hand, I mourn. Where does the Lord have a way? Who are the people He can use? What people on this earth afford Him a way?

We must turn to the Lord and ask for His mercy. Even if our gospel preaching is adequate, our Bible teaching accurate, and our meetings scriptural, we still need to ask ourselves: Do we have the ultimate move of God among us?

THE FOURTH STEP

There must be a good number, not just a few, who truly know how wonderful a Person Christ is. He must be our life, and we must live Him. We must be filled and permeated and saturated with Him. Our entire being must be infused with His feelings, His thoughts, and whatever He is. We must grow in life by being transformed little by little by His flowing life within us. Then we can be built up with our fellow believers. In our locality there will be a lampstand. The bride will be prepared for Him to come back. It is this that the Lord is after today. I call it the fourth step.

For the first step, the spread of the gospel, God prepared the Roman Empire. For the second step, the return to the Bible, God prepared Germany. For the third step, the recovery of the gospel, the teaching of the Bible, and the proper meetings—God in the last two centuries used Great Britain. Finally, for the fourth step God has prepared the United States. All of the big points of human history match God's move on the earth. Actually, all the major events of human history were prepared by God for His move on this earth.

THE PRESERVATION OF AMERICA

The continent of North America was created by God along with all the other continents. Yet it was concealed from the majority of mankind for thousands of years. God preserved it until His time was ripe. Then it was found by a new people, many of whom were God-loving and Bible-loving. These new, freethinking people founded a new nation. Surely these were not accidental events. Surely they did not happen without any meaning. The times have been appointed by God; the boundaries have been drawn by Him. The location of the United States, between two large oceans and in the temperate zone, is ideal. It is rich in natural resources.

We are here not by accident. Whether we were born here, or came here because of circumstances, our being here is by God's sovereign arrangement. When I was young, my family had considerable contact with American missionaries. We were quite westernized. From my youth I loved America. But

I had no thought of ever coming to this country. Nor did Brother Watchman Nee. Before 1950 none of us thought that our work would be in the Western World. We thought China was the field God had appointed to us. But God thought differently. He sovereignly brought the recovery to this country.

THE DECLINING QUALITY OF CHRISTIAN PUBLICATIONS

Some thirty-two years have passed since the recovery first went to Taiwan and then spread to the United States and the rest of the Western World. I have been observing the Christian publications these years. In the Chinese-speaking world hardly one book of spiritual weight has come out during this period. How about in Europe and in America? It is difficult to name one book with light and spiritual weight that has come out, like the ones that were published in the previous century.

One day in 1936 we were at a brother's house in Tientsin for lunch. Our work was being opposed, and Brother Nee was the target of their attack. At the dining table Brother Nee turned to me and said, "Witness, these people are opposing us, yet they still use our publications. I am going to stop our publications for a time. Let's see what other Christian groups will produce." And he did. In the years 1936 through 1938 there were nearly no publications by us. And in those few years no spiritual writings by others came out either.

THE SPREADING OF THE CENTRAL VISION

According to the present development of the world situation, the Lord will further isolate Gog and Magog (Russia). The Middle East is still a problem, but I believe in time the situation there also will result in the increased isolation of Russia. Russia's isolation will help the United States stay on top so that the world will be kept peaceful and free. For what? Not for the first century's spread of the gospel. Not for the Sixteenth Century's Reformation. Not for the Eighteenth and Nineteenth Centuries' Bible teaching and scriptural meetings. No! Rather, it is for the central vision of the Apostle Paul's completing ministry.

It is my earnest expectation that many saints will be burdened for this. Many, I hope, would be ready for the Lord's leading to go to other countries. Some may go to Athens, others to Jerusalem, others to Vienna and elsewhere, in order to spread the Lord's up-to-date, ultimate move on this earth.

THE FOUR GOSPELS

You will notice that the Scripture Reading at the beginning is from all four Gospels. Matthew says, "All authority has been given to Me....Go therefore and disciple all the nations..." (28:18-19). Matthew is for the kingdom, to disciple people to be citizens of the heavenly kingdom. Mark says, "Go ye into all the world, and preach the gospel to every creature" (16:15). The gospel is to be preached to every creature. Luke says, "That repentance and remission of sins should be preached in his name among all nations..." (24:47). Here the preaching is of repentance and forgiveness of sins in His name. The Gospel of John does not mention the preaching of the gospel. It says, "You did not choose Me, but I chose you, and I appointed you that you should go forth and bear fruit" (15:16). It is not a matter of preaching, but a matter of living to produce some fruit!

ACTS

After the four Gospels, there is the fifth book, Acts. Acts 1:8 says, "Ye shall receive power, after that the Holy Spirit is come upon you: and ye shall be witnesses unto me...." What is a witness? It is not just a preacher or an evangelist. It is the same word in Greek as martyr. A witness is a person bearing a testimony. The witness is the person; the testimony is the thing testified. On the day of Pentecost Peter and the others were not preachers so much as witnesses bearing the testimony. They were living persons, bearing the testimony of the One who had been incarnated, crucified, resurrected, and then had ascended and descended and who was still moving on this earth through His Body. They bore testimony to this Person. Their testimony was the gospel. It was not like the shallow gospel preached today: "You are a sinner. You deserve to go to hell. But God loves you. He sent His Son to be your

Savior. If you believe in Him, His blood will cleanse you from your sins, you will be forgiven, and you will go to heaven." This is the preaching of a shallow gospel, not the testimony borne by a witness. We are witnesses!

THE PREPARATION OF THE BRIDE

Then in the last book of the Bible, John, who had been there at Pentecost with Peter, said he was exiled "because of the word of God and the testimony of Jesus" (Rev. 1:9). What is this testimony? The testimony of Jesus is just the golden lampstand. John "testified the word of God and the testimony of Jesus Christ" (v. 2). We need to connect verse 2 with verse 12: "And I turned to see the voice that spoke with me; and having turned I saw seven golden lampstands." These lampstands were the testimony of Jesus. They were the churches (v. 20). Every church must be a golden lampstand, not merely an assembly of Christians meeting together in the name of Jesus. They must live Christ. They must become parts of Christ and have Christ become them. When they are gathered in a locality, they are a shining golden lampstand. This is the preparation of the bride.

Finally, there is Revelation 19:7: "Let us rejoice and exult, and let us give the glory to Him, for the marriage of the Lamb is come, and His wife has made herself ready." This is the last step, the ultimate move for God's desire. It is not just to have good gospel preaching, good Bible teaching, good scriptural meetings. It is rather that we have the reality of the two mysteries, Christ as the mystery of God (Col. 2:2) and the church as the mystery of Christ (Eph. 3:4).

God has surely prepared the United States for this very purpose. He is sovereignly ruling over the world situation. He has brought us to this country and supplied us that we may go out with His Word, spreading His ultimate move, that His eternal intention may be carried out.

Have I made this clear to you? When you meet the Lord, will you have any excuse that you did not understand? The Lord's recovery is not just a common piece of Christian work. Surely the Lord has shown us something of His ultimate move on this earth. You must bring what you have heard to the Lord and pray. You must fellowship with your wife or husband, with others who are close to you, again and again.

In many aspects Israel is ready for the Lord's coming back, but the church cannot yet match Israel. The world situation is all prepared, under the control of God's sovereign hand. He has made the United States the central and most convenient country, and He has placed us here. If you are keeping up-to-date with what is going on today on this earth, you will realize that God is controlling the entire world under the leadership of the United States for the spreading of His recovery.

You should not be here just to make a living! That is too low. Be burdened with God's ultimate move. Then you will see God's oneness with you, and there will be no problem with your living. I do not use the Old Testament term, that you will have God's blessing. I say that you will see God's oneness with you, because you are one with Him.

The time is short; the end is close. If you know world history and the trend of history, you will realize that it is unlikely God would prepare another country to be a power in this world for Him to take yet another step. I believe that America is the last power God will use for His final move. This fourth step, His final move, is the carrying out of His eternal intention to have a number of His seekers, lovers, live Christ and be the lampstand in their locality, that He may prepare His bride.

CHAPTER FIVE

GOD'S ULTIMATE MOVE, GOD'S ULTIMATE RECOVERY, AND THE WORLD'S ULTIMATE SITUATION

Scripture Reading: Col. 1:25-27; Eph. 1:20-23; 3:17a, 19b; John 14:23; 15:5; Rev. 2:7, 17; 3:12, 20; 1:4, 11-12, 20

Prayer: Lord, thank You for this gathering. You know the darkness of this age. You know how much we need light from You. Grant us the light from within. Open our eyes and open up the situation—the situation of today's world, the situation among today's Christians, and the situation of Your recovery. Lord, we claim the cleansing of Your precious blood. We thank You for such a covering which protects us from the enemy's attacks. Lord, be with us. Show us Your way. We are not content with knowledge. We want to see. Grant us a view, a vision. We thank You.

A CLEAR VIEW

God created the universe, the earth, and mankind. So whatever mankind's situation is on this earth must be under God's sovereign control. He had a purpose from the very beginning. In order to fulfill that purpose He created the universe and mankind. We know that the heavens are for the earth, the earth is for man, and man has a spirit to contact, receive, experience, and enjoy God (see Zech. 12:1).

We all need such a clear view from which to consider the world situation. The newspapers are not written from such a viewpoint! Historians do not have this view. They have studied mankind's situation. They have done research and perhaps even gotten doctoral degrees. Yet they do not know why mankind is on this earth.

I have spent over half a century in the Bible, in spiritual things, and in the church life. I have also been a student of world affairs since 1925. In that year I read a magazine, an authority on international affairs, which was published in Shanghai. It came out monthly, giving the Chinese people news concerning their country and the world. In it I read of the different pacts and treaties between China and other nations. From the very first issue I read, I was stirred up to take note of world affairs. That was the year I entered college. From that time on, I have kept informed of the world situation by reading the international news in the newspapers.

GOD'S ULTIMATE MOVE

The Lord is living and purposeful. His first move was to create the universe. "In the beginning God created the heaven and the earth" (Gen. 1:1). But what is His ultimate move? Some might answer that, according to Bible prophecy, before too long the Lord will come back to judge the world. Yes, this is in the Bible, but it is a doctrinal way of speaking; to speak in this way indicates a lack of light.

Recently I have had to work in my yard to change the dirt. The soil was clay, and the water did not drain. Even the most hardy plants were not growing well. I have had to spend much time to replace the soil and replant the shrubbery, but this was not my ultimate move. I also spent time cleaning up the yard and pruning some of the trees. But these were not my ultimate move either. My ultimate move is to come here and give you a message concerning God's ultimate move!

To say that the Lord Jesus will come back to clear up things on earth is true, just as it is true to say that I cleared up my yard. But clearing up things is not His ultimate move, just as it was not mine. God's ultimate move is to work Himself—Father, Son, and Spirit—into us and to become our life, that we may live Him out and express Him as His Body, the church.

Its Initiation

When did this ultimate move begin? It began with the incarnation of Jesus. A virgin named Mary became pregnant by the Holy Spirit coming upon her. This was the beginning. This is also the beginning of the New Testament. God entered into mankind! Then a little Child was born in the manger at Bethlehem. Isaiah 9:6 tells us that the Child was the mighty God. He was also the Son given; this Son of the Trinity was called the Father. Mysterious!

Its Development

When He was about thirty, He came out among the people. He was like a great magnet, drawing others after Him. As He walked along the seashore of Galilee, He saw Peter and Andrew fishing, and John and James mending their nets. When He called, "Come, follow Me!" they dropped their nets, left what they were doing, and followed this One, a carpenter (Matt. 4:18-22). What attracted them? I do not know, but there must have been something unusual about this young Man for them to leave everything and follow Him.

They spent three and a half years together. As the disciples stayed with Him more and more they realized how wonderful, excellent, and precious He was. Then one day He told them He was going away. He would be crucified and raised again on the third day (Matt. 16:21; 17:22-23). They could not understand. Though they had the Old Testament, prophesying His death and resurrection, they did not have the light. Though they had the words right from His mouth, they did not have the light.

Christ's Parting Words

On the last night before His crucifixion He told them that He was going away. He would be gone a short time in order to prepare the way to bring them all into the Father. He went on to say, "If anyone loves Me, he will keep My word, and My Father will love him, and We will come to him and make an abode with him" (John 14:23). They could not understand. Surely they were the best representatives of today's Christians. Yet they did not know or understand what the Lord was talking about.

In John 15 He went on to speak of Himself as the vine and the disciples as the branches. "Abide in Me and I in you," He told them (John 15:4). If you had been there, would you have understood what He meant? What kind of a vine can He be? How could I be a branch? Abide in Him? How could I get into Him to abide in Him? He abide in me? How could He get into me?

A New Language for a New Culture

Humankind had never heard such words. In human culture there had never been such language. But now there was coming into being a new culture. None of those there knew the language of the new culture. Crucified and resurrected after three days: here was something new in history. Then He would come back. The world would not see Him, but the disciples would. In that day they would know that He was in them (John 14:19-20). The Father would send the Spirit of reality who abode with them and would be in them (14:16-17). Did they not know that He was in the Father and the Father was in Him? To see Him was to see the Father. His words were not from Himself; His speaking was the Father's working (14:9-11). What language was this? It was the language of a new culture being formed. Though the disciples had not experienced this culture, the language was there describing it.

What the Lord said happened. He went to the cross, died, and then was resurrected the third day. That very morning some of the women discovered something new in this culture. The One who had been buried was no longer in the tomb; it was empty. He talked with these women. Many exciting things happened that day. By evening when the disciples met together, they were afraid. Suddenly, with no knock on the door, this Jesus was there standing in their midst (John 20:19)! "Peace be to you," He said. They must have been shocked. Then He breathed into them and said, "Receive the Holy *Pneuma*" (v. 22). He entered into them and never left. He was now one with them. When they went fishing, He was there.

After fifty days, Pentecost came. While the disciples were together, He poured Himself out upon them (Acts 2:1-4). Now He was not only within them; He was upon them as well. They were baptized into one Body. They acted in a crazy way, these people who were experiencing something pre-history.

They had everything in common (2:44). When we are crazy, we do not care for our own things; others can take whatever they want of ours. When we are sober, we know what is ours. "This is my refrigerator. You have no right to open it. This is my bread. You may not help yourself to it." At Pentecost the disciples were beside themselves. "Here, take whatever you like. Help yourself to whatever you would like to eat or drink." But, such an attitude does not indicate that they were spiritual. Communal living is childish, although many Christians like to copy that. In China there was a group called The Jesus Family. Those who joined them had to sell everything and put every cent into the common account. This does not mean very much; it is not the Lord's move. Before too long, quarreling arises. Some get too much food; others get too little. In a short time the communal life in the book of Acts was over. The Holy Spirit did not care for that.

Even the Apostle Peter was not clear about God's ultimate move! I say this because in his writings and messages he gives no hint of it. He does not tell us that Christ lives in us. Perhaps his best phrase is that we are "partakers of the divine nature" (2 Pet. 1:4).

Besides the Lord Himself in John 14:23 and 15:4-5, only Paul clearly and strongly tells us that Christ is our life, that He lives in us, and that He even makes His home in us. Colossians 1:25-27 says, "Of which I became a minister according to the stewardship of God, which was given to me for you, to complete the word of God, the mystery which has been hidden from the ages and from the generations, but now has been manifested to His saints; to whom God willed to make known what are the riches of the glory of this mystery among the nations, which is Christ in you, the hope of glory." Paul here says that he was commissioned to complete the word of God. This completion is the mystery that Christ lives in us.

In Ephesians Paul prays for the believers "to be strengthened with power through His Spirit into the inner man, that Christ may make His home in your hearts...that you may be filled unto all the fullness of God (3:16-17, 19). What language is this? It is the language of the new culture, a culture

never before heard of in the world's history! In the first chapter Paul tells the saints that this dear One who will make
home in them has been raised from the dead, uplifted to the
heavens far above all, and made Head over all things to
the church; all things have been subjected under His feet
(1:20-22). He is Head not only *for* the church but *to* the church,
which is His Body, the fullness of the One who fills all in all
(vv. 22-23). Here is a new language. Even after more than
1900 years most Christians still do not understand it.

If you ask Christians about Christ making His home in
their hearts or about the church as His Body being the fullness of Him who fills all in all, many will wonder what you
are talking about. They have heard of hell and the heavenly
mansions. They understand joy and peace. But the language
of Paul is foreign to them. This is a heavenly, eternal language, describing something new in human history.

Defined in Paul's Writings

The Bible clearly tells us what God's ultimate move is.
God's ultimate move is to have Christ as the mystery of God
enter into us as our life. Then we become His living members
and together form His Body, which is the very fullness of the
One who fills all in all. We do not understand this in an adequate way, but this is what is in the Bible. This is Paul's
completing ministry, telling us that Christ is God's mystery
and Christ has become our life; that we are the church, which
is Christ's mystery (Eph. 3:4-6); that the church is the Body.
No other writer of the Bible besides Paul tells us that the
church is the Body of Christ.

Strengthened in John's Writings

But Paul's ministry was damaged. Even before his death, a
decline had set in. Different teachings came in. Thus Paul
wrote in 1 Timothy about holding the mystery of the faith
(3:9). What is the mystery? "Great is the mystery of godliness, Who was manifested in the flesh, vindicated in the
Spirit, seen by angels, preached among the nations, believed
on in the world, taken up in glory" (3:16). This was Paul's

declaration to bring the degraded Christians back to his completing ministry.

Later God raised up the oldest apostle, John, and gave him the mending ministry. (We have already published three series of messages on this, called The Heavenly Ministry of Christ, The Completing Ministry of Paul, and The Mending Ministry of John.) John's Gospel, Epistles, and Revelation were all written around A.D. 90. These last books of the Bible were written to mend the broken net, the broken completing ministry.

What was the way to mend? It was to say the same thing. We have already mentioned John 14 and 15, where the Lord Jesus said He and the Father would make Their abode with us, and that He would be in us and we in Him. He also said that we may eat Him as the living bread (John 6:51) and live because of Him (v. 57). In his Epistles he tells us repeatedly that God dwells in us (1 John 3:24b; 4:13, 15, 16).

Then in Revelation the Lord Jesus Himself promised, "To him who overcomes...I will give to eat of the tree of life" (2:7); "To him who overcomes...I will give of the hidden manna" (2:17). He promised eating of the tree of life and of the hidden manna and feasting with Him (3:20). He also promised, "He who overcomes, I will make him a pillar in the temple of My God" (3:12). A pillar is for building. Thus the eating of Christ is for the building. At the end of Revelation, that is, at the end of the entire Bible, what will there be? A built-up Jerusalem with the throne, the river of life, and the tree of life growing along the two sides of the river. This is a clear picture of the coming consummation of God's purpose. This is God's ultimate move. We all have to see this.

Some Christians say that they follow Christ, not Paul. What can this mean? Such preaching will be largely limited to these points: Christ is the Son of God; He became a man, lived on this earth, then died on the cross for our sins; He was buried, then arose from the dead, and is now on the throne; He is our Redeemer and Savior, soon to return to take us to heaven; by believing in Him we have forgiveness of sins and are children of God; while we are on this earth, we have to improve our behavior that our lives may glorify God.

At best, Christian teachers today just encourage people to love God and to go out to win souls. They do not realize that the fourth Gospel was written by John to mend Paul's broken ministry. How could they say they follow Christ? If they follow Christ, they should follow His word in John 14 and 15. They also should follow His word in Revelation, "To him who overcomes, to him I will give to eat of the tree of life, which is in the paradise of God." This is Christ's word. But it seems that in their Bible the book of Revelation is missing. In their theology they do not have the seven Spirits. Nor do they have Christ in resurrection becoming the life-giving Spirit and indwelling us.

Although many Christians appreciate the Nicene Creed, it has some defects. These two main points are clearly stated in the New Testament: (1) Paul's Epistles tell us that Christ in resurrection became the life-giving Spirit indwelling us (1 Cor. 15:45; 2 Tim. 4:22); (2) John's writings tell us of the seven Spirits for the seven golden lampstands (Rev. 1:4, 11-12, 20). But the Nicene Creed did not cover these two things. Many Christians believe that this creed, made under Constantine the Great, is scriptural and fundamental. But, it neglects what Paul tells us in his completing ministry, that Christ lives in us that we may all become His Body. It ignores what John tells us in his mending ministry, that Christ lives in us to be our food, the tree of life, the manna, even a feast, that we may become a lampstand.

In the Scriptures only Paul tells us that the church is the Body of Christ; only John tells us that the church is a lampstand. To be the Body and to be the lampstand both depend upon the eating of Jesus.

These Christians who claim to follow Christ but not Paul remind me of the primitive missionaries who went to China. What message did these missionaries mainly have? Only "Jesus loves me, this I know, for the Bible tells me so!" They had no hymn about Christ making His home in my heart. They had no hymn saying that Jesus, after resurrection, became a life-giving Spirit to live in me to be my life that I might be His member and all of us might be His Body, the church, the fullness of Him who fills all in all.

I hope some hymns could be written, saying that Christ is now the life-giving Spirit, even the seven Spirits, in me to make me His living member; this I know because the Bible tells me so!

A popular Bible teacher has said that since these two trees, the tree of life and the tree of the knowledge of good and evil are not here now, there is no reason to be concerned about them. He did not realize that these two trees are here within us more than they were in the garden of Eden! In the garden they were outside Adam; today they are within us. Is not the tree of life in you? Is not the tree of the knowledge of good and evil in you? Paul says, "Christ [who is the real tree of life] lives in me" (Gal. 2:20). Paul also says, "If what I do not will, this I do, it is no longer I that do it but sin that dwells in me" (Rom. 7:20). Who is this sin? It is Satan in our flesh (7:17-18) who is the real tree of the knowledge of good and evil. If the tree of life is not in you, how could you have the law of the Spirit of life? If the tree of knowledge is not in you, how could you have the law of sin and death (8:2; 7:21)? Do you see the blindness, the ignorance, the superficiality, of most of today's Christian teachings?

GOD'S ULTIMATE RECOVERY

What is the Lord's ultimate recovery? The initial recovery was in the time of Martin Luther. What is the ultimate recovery? Is it to recover the communal life? Is it to recover the washing of feet? Foot-washing is in the Bible, but foot-washing is not the Lord's ultimate recovery.

The Lord's ultimate recovery is the same as the Lord's ultimate move. That is, He wants to recover Christ, the mystery of God, becoming the indwelling Spirit to infuse, impart, the Triune God into the tripartite man, thus making us who believe in Him members of His Body for His expression. This Body is expressed locally as the lampstand, which becomes His testimony, the testimony of Jesus.

The ultimate move of God has been lost sight of. Now the Lord is going to recover it. Three to four hundred years ago some matters were recovered by the Puritans, but the points were not as great as what Zinzendorf and John Nelson Darby saw. The Brethren saw something great, but they became centered on doctrines and were killed by the letter of the Bible. What the Lord is going to recover is simply this: Christ as the mystery of God to live in us as the indwelling Spirit, making us His members that we may become the church, the mystery of Christ, as the Body to express Him. This expression is the lampstand.

After the Lord recovers this, He will have completed what He intended to do. This is as far as God went while Paul was on earth. How could He recover more than this? God is now recovering this last item among us: Christ in you, the hope of glory, making us all His living Body.

KEPT FROM DISTRACTIONS

If you see this, you will never be led astray. Nothing will distract you. It is because I have seen what the Lord's ultimate move is that I have been kept in the recovery over a half century. I have been kept, not because the churches were always wonderful, not because the co-workers were always pleasant. What has held me is my seeing of the Lord's ultimate recovery from the very first day I started on this way. In the twenty years I have been with you, I have never changed my tone. If the Lord grants me another twenty-five years, I should be able to finish the Life-study of the entire Bible. Then you will see that all the Life-studies are on the same subject: the two great mysteries, the mystery of God (Christ) and the mystery of Christ (the church). All of you need to see this. Do not be preoccupied with anything else. Focus instead on this ultimate move of God.

THE PREPARATION IN CHINA

In the past two centuries God sent the finest spiritual missionaries to China. Hudson Taylor was one; his experience of John 15 was rare. Another was Mr. Woodbury, who set up a Christian and Missionary Alliance Church in Shanghai around 1920. In the years after that, spiritual seekers realized that that was the most spiritual mission that went to China. One medical student he helped was a Dr. Lee, who became an outstanding spiritual native. He knew the cross and the resurrection life. Then there was also Miss M. E. Barber, who helped Brother Watchman Nee. Through her we became acquainted with the spiritual writings from the West. How could we have been in a faraway, backward country and still have gotten to know spiritual books that even some of you are not familiar with? It was through these top spiritual persons.

In 1927 Brother Watchman Nee began to write *The Spiritual Man*. In this book he has many translations from the writings of others. In the preface of the first Chinese edition Brother Nee indicated this. It was more than fifty years ago that Brother Nee translated these spiritual writings into Chinese and made them available to us. Neither Brother Nee nor I had been to the Western World, but by the Lord's sovereignty we went to English-speaking colleges. We read in English the history of the church, the biographies and autobiographies of the spiritual giants of the past, and the central themes of the great writers.

When Paul was still Saul, before he was called to the completing ministry, he had been taught the Old Testament at the feet of Gamaliel (Acts 22:3). I am grateful for what I learned from the great Brethren teachers on the Old Testament and on prophecy. Many of the messages I have given on the tabernacle and on the ark were based on their teachings. Though their teaching was just in a doctrinal way, it was correct. After all these years, I have gained some experiences. I do not like to teach the types in a doctrinal way, but rather to apply them to our experience. But, we owe much to the Brethren teachers; we are on their shoulders.

If such missionaries had not been sent to China, how could we have become Christians? Less than two centuries ago the blood of Christ's Body flowed to China and produced new cells. Now it has flowed back to the Western World. I am sorry to say that due to pride many Christians refuse to take what has come back. But thank the Lord, many have taken it.

THE WORLD'S ULTIMATE SITUATION

The Lord raised up Great Britain and used her for more

than two centuries to spread the gospel and the spiritual teachings. Now, however, America has come into the lead.

A New Country for the Lord's Move

Until five hundred years ago, this continent lay hidden, a virgin land. Why did God preserve this continent for so long? No historian has said this, but my answer is that God arranged this so that America would be preserved for His ultimate recovery. About 1500 the Lord exposed this new continent to the people of Europe, who were the most advanced. At that very time, there were many thoughtful persons who loved the Lord. They wanted to be free in their thinking about spiritual things. The Catholic Church and the state churches, however, were persecuting them. Even in England some thoughtful persons who loved the Bible were burned at the stake by the Church of England. Thus, many lovers of the Lord aspired to come to the new land. As time went on, many came and eventually a new country was founded.

The United States is different from any other country. It is constitutional and democratic. It offers freedom of speech and of religion. This is why we can speak so freely here. Because of its good foundation, Americans are generally frank and open to new things. It does not matter to them who offers them something; he may be Chinese, or Indian, or Black. As long as what he offers is better, they will take it! This is not so with Britain, France, or any other leading countries. America is different. It is a melting pot, melting not only different peoples but different cultures as well. America takes the best things of different cultures. If I were in other countries, I might not be received so well. But here, even though I am opposed, close to ten thousand have accepted the Lord's recovery. The way I speak English does not bother them. Americans care for the facts. Is any other country like this? The United States is extraordinary.

Through two world wars God put down Britain and raised up the United States. If the United States had not intervened in World War I, it is doubtful that Britain and France could have won. After that war, Britain and France formed the League of Nations in order to restrict Germany. The United

States was not a member. In World War II the United States was mainly responsible for the defeat of Germany in Europe and of Japan in the Pacific. Roosevelt proposed that all the different peoples, even though small in number, be given their freedom. There would be no more colonies. Britain had to agree. Then the United Nations was formed in San Francisco. Its headquarters were set up in the UN Building in New York with the help of the United States.

The Containment of Russia

Gradually, after these two world wars, the whole world came under the influence of the United States. The only exception is Russia, Gog and Magog; this fulfills what the Bible says. They resist God and preach atheism. Mr. Franklin D. Roosevelt was a great statesman, but he made mistakes. One was to recognize Russia, when all the other nations had been refusing to have diplomatic relations with her. This he did in 1933. Then, during the second World War, he sent supplies to Russia to help defeat Germany. Russia should not have been given this much help. The United States should have let Germany and Russia exhaust each other. As it was, Russia became stronger because of this mistake and became a problem to the United States after the war. The Marshall Plan, which helped the Western European countries recover from the war, was rejected by the Soviet Union. She did not want help for herself or her satellites because she feared interference in her internal affairs. Roosevelt made a third mistake by signing the secret Yalta agreements, which further spread Russian influence. But God is sovereign.

Just in these last few days the newspapers have reported that China's premier has been upheld in his plan to continue China's ties with the West. We might imagine that a Communist country like Red China would side with Russia against the free world, but the policy it is adopting will serve instead to isolate Russia. They have also sent envoys to contact India and Pakistan concerning the isolation of Russia.

Until some twenty years ago Russia had no access to the oceans. Now she has expanded her navy and has a free way on the Pacific Ocean. She has gotten the use of Qui Non Bay in Vietnam, where there is a huge naval base built by the United States during the Vietnam war; now it has fallen into Russian hands. This is why America's Seventh Fleet is needed in the Pacific to safeguard the free world's interests.

These recently reported moves which will further isolate Russia are part of the world's ultimate situation. The raising up of America as the top nation is also part of this final stage. If you are familiar with world history and have seen the tendencies of mankind, you will surely agree that there is no possibility of another nation being raised up to succeed the United States. What other country could it be? In Europe? In Asia? In Africa? In Australasia? This situation of the United States in the lead and Russia being increasingly isolated is the ultimate situation. Its purpose is the carrying out of the Lord's ultimate recovery.

Israel and the Church

Israel has been re-formed. Jerusalem is in Israeli hands. Though in many aspects Israel is ready for the Lord's coming back, the church is not. Can the church be prepared in Catholicism or Protestantism? I can see no evidence that it can. I have not heard of any book or person of spiritual weight coming out of America or Europe these past twenty years. The situation in the world and the condition of Christianity are like puzzle pieces. If you fit them together, you will realize that the Lord's move today is the recovery. He will use this last world situation, that is, the supremacy of the United States, for the spreading of the recovery. No other country is so central, so convenient, and so prevailing as the United States. The U.S.A. is so good for the Lord's recovery and so good for the spreading of the recovery.

OUR RESPONSIBILITY

All that is needed is our faithfulness. We all have to be faithful; we all must seek after Him. We must treasure this time in which we live. We must treasure the vision of the recovery. And we must treasure our responsibility. Just forget about everything else. Rise up and stand for the Lord's recovery. This is the ultimate time for God to accomplish His purpose to bring the Lord back.

Living Stream Ministry
2431 W. La Palma Ave.
Anaheim, CA 92801
714-991-4681

Thu, Mar 2, 2017 10:10 am

OTC Sale 1216272690.2 R956 P1705

| 04-010-401   1 @ 3.88 ==> | 3.88 |
| World Situation and God's Move, The | |

	Sub Total	3.88
	7.75% Sales Tax	0.30
	Total	**4.18**
Account 3378 Ref H21201		4.18
	Change Due	0.00

Total Items: 1

Thank You
Visit www.lsm.org for online
publications, Life-Study of the Bible
broadcasts, and more.

CHAPTER SIX

GOD'S ULTIMATE RECOVERY
AND THE WORLD'S ULTIMATE SITUATION

Scripture Reading: Rev. 1:1, 2, 11-18, 20; 2:7; 3:12; 4:5; 5:6; 19:7-8; 22:1-2, 14, 17

THE IMPORTANCE OF PAUL'S WRITINGS

God's ultimate move was fully revealed through one apostle, Paul. He was the one who received the stewardship to complete the word of God (Col. 1:25-27), that is, to complete the revelation of God's move.

Without Paul's Epistles we can see God's move in creation. We can also see His move in incarnation. The four Gospels tell us how God in the Person of the Son became incarnate. They also reveal His move in crucifixion and in resurrection. To some extent they also show God's move in ascension. The book of Acts goes on to show more: how God moved by descending upon the disciples and by setting up the churches. However, with Acts there is no completion of the revelation of God's move.

In order to see God's ultimate activities in relation to mankind, we must go beyond Acts to the fourteen Epistles of the Apostle Paul. He clearly presents this ultimate move: the Triune God, having passed through many processes, is now working Himself into His chosen people to be their life. He is now the indwelling Spirit. This Spirit is the consummate expression and reaching to man of the Triune God, that He may constitute His chosen people both the sons of God with the divine life and nature and also the members of Christ organically united to Him, so that God may have a family and Christ may have a Body to express Him corporately.

Does any New Testament writer other than Paul give us this revelation? Peter's writings say nothing of this. We treasure Peter's Epistles mainly because of his word about our being "partakers of the divine nature" (2 Pet. 1:4). Peter has written only eight chapters, five in his first Epistle and three in his second. He mentions the burning of the old creation and the coming of a new heaven and a new earth. But nowhere does he tell us that Christ lives in us. He never mentions that we are members of Christ. He does not even tell us that the church is the Body of Christ. These are not insignificant items. They are great! Since Peter does not mention them, he must not have seen them very clearly.

Paul covers all these matters not just in one or two verses but in fourteen books. He tells us that we have been not only justified and reconciled to God, but also that we have been born of Him! We are His sons, possessing His life and nature. This means we are of the same nature as God. If our children have our life and nature, are they not the same as we are? They are not we, yet they are the same as we. We are not God, yet we are the same as God in the divine life and nature. We are sons born of Him, not sons adopted by Him. Paul made this more than clear.

He also made clear that we are the members of Christ. He said it was of God that we are in Christ (1 Cor. 1:30). We were in Adam, but God has transferred us into Christ, not just in a positional way but in a living way. Thus there is an organic union between us and Christ. We are His members. He is the Head; we are the Body. He and we are both Christ. The corporate Christ is not only the Head, but also the Body. How could someone have a head and no body? Yet this is the Christ of many Christians. They do not even think of Christ as having a Body. Many Christians lack a direct realization that we are members of Christ. Do you have such a sense? Paul even says that our bodies are members of Christ (1 Cor. 6:15). Not only our spirit but our body! To be one with Christ, to be His Body, is a great matter. Where did this revelation come from? No one but Paul made this so clear. He completed the revelation of the divine Word, telling us that God's ultimate move is to get this Body, this large family.

JOHN'S WRITINGS

Unfortunately, this revelation was damaged. So after the completing ministry, God gave the mending ministry. John came in to mend. When the sisters repair a hole in an article of clothing, they make the mended part stronger than the original. This is also true to some extent of John's ministry. Paul, for example, does not tell us of the seven Spirits. Is God's Spirit one or seven? The Spirit is both one and seven. The mender stresses the Spirit sevenfold more than Paul. John also tells us that the seven Spirits are the eyes of the Lamb (Rev. 5:6). If the Trinity comprises three separate Persons, how can the Third be the eyes of the Second? How could this be explained? No one can analyze the Trinity. Paul, however, firstly tells us that Christ in resurrection became a life-giving Spirit (1 Cor. 15:45b). Then John indicates that this life-giving Spirit is the seven Spirits. He strengthens the Spirit sevenfold. This is just one example of how the mending ministry is stronger than the completing.

THE LEAKAGE AND THE BEGINNING OF THE RECOVERY

The Bible was completed by the end of the first century. The final books were John's writings—the Gospel, the Epistles, and Revelation. But from that time a leakage began because the vessel became broken. It continued through the second and third centuries and on, until by the end of the sixth century the Catholic Church and the papal system were fully established.

The years from about A.D. 500 to 1500 are called the Dark Ages. All the truths in the New Testament had leaked away. The Bible itself was locked up. The common people were told that they were not in a position nor did they have the capability to read the Scriptures; they needed the pope and the Church to interpret it for them. For a thousand years there was darkness. Then the Reformation began, with Martin Luther boldly taking the lead.

The Reformation marks the beginning of the recovery. Do you know what book the recovery began with? It was Romans, the first book of Paul's completing ministry. Luther, however, did not recover everything in Romans. We have since seen far more. But we do not despise him. In his time he was a person to be really appreciated. He had the boldness to declare that justification is by faith. That was the beginning of the Lord's recovery. Following justification by faith, one truth after another was recovered. This is the reason many seeking Christians began to dispute with each other. Because one would see one thing and another something else, each would fight for what he had seen. Many things were recovered. But, until these recent years none of the items in the verses listed at the beginning of this message were recovered.

ITEMS IN THE ULTIMATE RECOVERY

From these verses we now see that the church in a locality is a lampstand and that each city has only one lampstand (Rev. 1:11-18, 20). Did you ever hear that Christ has promised to give the overcomer to eat of the tree of life (2:7)? Many Christians think the tree of life was only in Genesis and has nothing to do with us today. Did you ever hear that you could be a pillar in God's temple and that you could bear the name of God, and of the New Jerusalem, and the new name of Christ (3:12)? Did you ever hear that God's Spirit is one but has become seven (4:5)? Even we were not so clear about this before 1969! Did you ever hear that these seven Spirits who are the one Spirit of God are the eyes of the redeeming Lamb (5:6)? Did you ever hear a message that the Lamb's marriage is come and His wife has made herself ready (19:7-8)? Did you ever hear a message on the spiritual significance of the New Jerusalem, with the throne of God, the flowing river, and the tree of life (22:1-2)? Did you ever hear of the enjoyment of Christ as life by those who wash their robes and thus have the right to the tree of life (22:14)? Did you ever hear "the Spirit and the bride say" together (22:17)? You may have heard Christ and the church linked together, but probably you have not heard the Spirit and the bride linked together.

All these items are different aspects of the Lord's ultimate recovery. Many of them have been recovered just within these past thirty years, some of them in the United States. Yet they are all in the Bible, especially in the last book of the Bible.

They simply remained there, untouched. Five hundred years ago, it was the same with justification by faith. It was there in Romans and Galatians, yet not understood or touched by most of the so-called Christians. Revelation was considered mysterious; it seemed better to leave it alone.

THE BIBLE UNLOCKED AND THEN OPENED

About the same time as the Reformation, movable type was invented in Europe. I am talking about the recovery with the world situation because these two things go together. The reformers made use of the printing press to publish the truths they had seen. The Bible also could be printed instead of being copied by hand. As a result, it was spread among the people. Formerly it had been locked up by the Catholic Church. Martin Luther unlocked it. But the Bible was not opened up much; it was read but not really understood.

It was not till 1830 or so that the great teachers among the Brethren opened up the Bible much more. They came to understand the types and prophecies and the matter of Christ's second coming in a general way. Gradually the prophecies in Revelation were opened up. But some matters in Revelation they ignored: they did not touch the testimony of Jesus, the lampstands, the seven Spirits, the tree of life, and the spiritual significance of the New Jerusalem. What they studied was mostly the seven seals, the seven trumpets, the seven bowls, the seven heads, and the ten horns. They were scholars, showing that many of the prophecies were historically fulfilled. The Brethren gave us many basic interpretations of the Bible.

THE NEW LIGHT IN THE RECOVERY

Revelation opens with "the revelation of Jesus Christ" (1:1). Revelation is not only an objective term; it has a subjective aspect as well. It is a revelation not only by Christ, but also of Him. The Revelation of Jesus Christ is like a photograph of Him.

The Jesus Christ in Revelation 1 is altogether different from the One described in the four Gospels! John in his youth had leaned upon the Lord's bosom (John 13:23). Now in his old age he was terrified by the Jesus he saw (Rev. 1:17). The

Christ who is described in Revelation is even different from the Christ in Paul's revelation. In Colossians Paul revealed a Christ who is everything—He is all-inclusive; He is all-extensive; He is the portion of the saints; He is the image of God; He is the first item of all the creatures; He is the Firstborn of resurrection; He is the reality of all the shadows! To most Christians Jesus is only meek and gentle. But in Revelation this all-inclusive, extensive Christ becomes so terrifying.

The Seven Spirits

It is not a light matter that in our day and among us the Lord has recovered these things. The matter of the seven Spirits was recovered in the Erie conference in the summer of 1969. On my way to one of the meetings of the conference I still did not know what I should speak on. As I walked toward the meeting place, the title "The Seven Spirits" came to me. Before that, I had no thought of speaking on that subject. After I had given the message, one of the brothers told me that of all the messages he had heard me give, this one was the most living. Afterwards, I went back to Los Angeles for the conference and training. That time of training in 1969 was the high point of the Lord's recovery in the United States. Those messages were a continuation of the subject of the seven Spirits.

The Tree of Life

In these past twenty years I have said many times that you should eat of the tree of life. In fact, the first stage of my stay in this country might be considered the tree-of-life stage! I have given several messages pointing out the correspondence between the first two chapters of the Bible and the last two chapters. Some have been caught for the Lord's recovery by hearing a message on the two trees and on the New Jerusalem.

The Lampstand and the Building

Before I left mainland China in 1949, these topics were not adequately mentioned. Not only has the church been recovered, but the church specifically as the lampstand.

Besides the eating of the tree of life, the building has also been recovered. The King James Version uses the word edifying instead of building; to most people to be edified means to be instructed, not to be built up. Many times I have spoken to you on the building. We have published a book called *Life and Building as Portrayed in the Song of Songs;* this book came from messages given in Los Angeles in 1972. Also, when we had the training on the Gospel of John, I pointed out that this Gospel deals with life and building. To my knowledge no one before us ever called attention to the matter of building in John's Gospel.

Final Items

What a privilege to be here today! Even twenty years ago we did not have so much light on the tree of life for God's building. When we were on the mainland of China, we seldom mentioned the matter of God's building, but since coming to the U.S.A., many messages have been given on the river of life and the tree of life in Revelation 22:1-2 for God's building. I have spoken many times on the Bible's concluding with a promise (22:14) and a call (22:17). Don't think that I speak on these matters as a hobby. No! I have a burden. What is there left to recover after the New Jerusalem with the river of life and the tree of life for God's building? The Lord's recovery began with Romans. It will conclude with Revelation.

What can come after these: the revelation of Jesus Christ, the testimony of Jesus, the lampstand, the eating of the tree of life, the seven Spirits, God's building, the New Jerusalem with the river of life flowing and the tree of life growing in the river, the promise to eat and the call to drink? Do you not realize that these are the items comprising the ultimate recovery?

NOT A WAY BUT A VISION

Recently some of the leading ones asked me how the churches should go on. I told them frankly that to ask for a way to go on is to ask for more religion. Every way is a religion. If Brother Lawrence's *Practice of the Presence of God* is merely a way, it is a religion. The same is true of Thomas a

Kempis' *Imitation of Christ*. The attempt to imitate Christ by killing the self is asceticism; it is not really a bearing of the cross. If what Madame Guyon experienced was merely a way, it was the religion of mysticism. Among ourselves some fifty years ago we practiced reckoning. If that was merely a way, it also was a religion. In 1939 Brother Watchman Nee began to see more of the Spirit in Romans 8. After that, he said that we could not experience the death of Christ as long as we were in Romans 6; we had to be in Romans 8. It is through the Spirit, not through our reckoning. If we depend on reckoning, we simply have a reckoning religion. You may ask, What is *not* a religion? The life-giving Spirit! The seven Spirits!

When the children of Israel traveled through the wilderness, they had no way. They followed the cloud, the Spirit. They followed the high priest's contact with God in the Holy of Holies. When the high priest went into the Holy of Holies to contact God, on his breast was a plate with precious stones bearing all the names of the twelve tribes. This plate was like a typewriter. Through it the priest knew what God wanted them to do; it was not by written regulations. Today if we want to know what to do, where to go, or what to say, we do not go according to some verse in the Bible, but according to the Spirit. Romans 8 tells us this. The righteous requirement of the law will be fulfilled in us, who do not walk according to flesh, but according to spirit (v. 4). And we must realize that the wonderful Christ is in our spirit.

It is not a matter of learning a way. We must come to see the vision! We must see the last recovery of the Lord! These messages are just to unveil to you the Lord's ultimate recovery. The Lord does not want other things. He wants nothing except to have Himself wrought into you.

THE ULTIMATE WORLD SITUATION

In previous chapters we have covered how the Lord arranged the proper situation for the carrying out of His move. He prepared the Roman Empire for the accomplishment of redemption and for the spread of the gospel. For the Reformation He raised up Germany. For the gospel to be spread to all parts of the earth He raised up Great Britain.

For the Lord to achieve His ultimate move He also needs the proper situation. If you consider the entire world today, you would have to say that the best place for the spreading of His recovery is the United States of America. We labored on the mainland of China from 1922 to 1949. Many were gained; many churches were raised up. Then from 1949 the whole of China began to be closed to us. I was sent out, and many of my co-workers were put into prison. It was a grief and disappointment to me. Now, however, I am no longer disappointed. In fact, I am greatly encouraged.

The Best Language

I can see that if all the items of the recovery were only in the Chinese language, they would lie buried, unavailable to those who did not know Chinese. What is printed in Chinese is preserved, but it does not spread. The best language for the spreading of the truth is American English. Within two weeks after a message is given, it can be sent to all five continents in a universally understood language by printed page, by audio tapes, and by video tapes.

The Best Place

Through all of human history there has never been such a country as the United States. How I thank the Lord for such a country where there is freedom of speech, a democratic, constitutional government, all the modern conveniences, and an abundance of resources! Forty-five years ago I was in the interior of China, traveling, preaching, teaching the Bible. I traveled by mule wagon over poor roads. From early morning till late in the evening we were on the road, yet we covered at most thirty miles. There is no comparison between that and the way the word can be spread today throughout the whole world from the United States. Planes fly from here to any part of the globe in less than twenty-four hours. Telephone connects us with Europe, Asia, Africa, and Australasia. Publications and cassette tapes are easily sent abroad. The recovery will spread. Sooner or later, these truths will be adopted. Just as justification by faith spread, so the truth of the tree of life will spread.

TRENDS IN HISTORY

When I came to this country in 1958, there were some who were predicting the downfall of the United States. They said that the United States was following the pattern of the Roman Empire, becoming corrupt and bankrupt. I argued against them. The United States was established on a different foundation. It is the only great power in history that has not robbed other countries. It is built upon its own resources and its own people. Because of its vast riches, it has no need to rob others. After my visit here in 1958, I went on to Europe. I found that in England, Denmark, and the other northern European countries there was the expectation that Communism would take over. Again I boldly argued that this would not be the case.

The oil crisis did not occur till 1973, but in 1962 I told the brothers that in the Mideast the problems would be the oil. I told them that the nations would not be able to resolve this problem and that God would do something about it. This was not a prophecy; it was just a talk I had with the brothers over twenty years ago.

THE LAST COUNTRY FOR THE LAST MOVE

Almost every part of the globe is being used, and natural resources are close to an end. Can humankind last another few centuries? Is there time for the Lord to raise up another world power after the United States? I do not believe so. It seems that the United States is the last power raised up by the Lord to match His recovery.

As this ultimate move of the Lord goes forward from here, there is the need for such a powerful country to keep the world at peace and to keep the way open. Now that we have planes like the 747s, we no longer need the Roman roads that were used in the early centuries for the spread of the gospel. But these 747s need a peaceful situation for the word of the Lord's recovery to go out. If the peace is broken, the spread will be stopped. The Lord needs a country for this. The United States, instead of robbing other countries, has been a giver. Since the end of the war in 1945, the United States has given away billions of dollars to other countries. You may be concerned that the deficit is getting bigger; however, the money the government owes is mostly to its own people. This is like a father owing money to his sons. The account shows red; but the money being spent is in the family.

If your eyes are open, you will realize what an age and what a country you live in, what the Lord's recovery is, and how the world situation is going on. The state of things today is for one thing—the Lord's recovery. The world is going on for the spreading of the recovery, for the preparing of the bride, for the lampstands to be raised up and shining in many countries. In this ultimate recovery what the Lord is regaining is not small teachings but big items, especially from the viewpoint of the central vision. This is the Lord's ultimate recovery, and He has such a country to maintain the world situation that His recovery may be spread.

CHAPTER SEVEN

OUR ULTIMATE RESPONSIBILITY

Scripture Reading: John 15:5, 16a; Acts 1:8; 1 Cor. 2:1-2; 6:17; Phil. 1:20-21a; Eph. 4:4a; Col. 3:10-11; Rev. 1:2, 11, 12; 19:7, 8

GOD'S HAND IN WORLD AFFAIRS

In previous messages we have seen God's ultimate move, God's ultimate recovery, and the world's ultimate situation. Now we have to realize our responsibility related to these three things. My burden is not to talk about politics but to show you that since God has a purpose to accomplish on this earth with mankind, He surely has the sovereign authority and power to arrange the situations in human history. I don't believe that many of the professors who teach world history know the significance in human history. Most of them only have the knowledge according to the world's knowledge. Surely not many have any concept that the world situation has so much to do with God's move.

Actually, the world situation is under the arrangement of God. It is God who appointed the times for a certain race to do this or to be there. It is God who made the borders of all the different nations (Acts 17:26). It is God who raised up kings and who put down nations. This is clear not only from the Bible but also from the historical facts.

AN AWARENESS OF HUMAN AFFAIRS

When I studied world history in college, our textbook covered the subject only till about 1920. It was published before 1925. As I have mentioned, I have been observing the world situation since 1925. My knowledge has come, not from textbooks, but from magazines, newspapers, and my own observation. For example, in September 1939 my brother came to ask me about the exchange rate and other matters that suddenly became problems to him in the export business he was in. What caused these hardships? Hitler had invaded Poland, causing the outbreak of World War II. The export business, of course, is much involved with the international situation. I mention this to illustrate how aware we were of world affairs. I have followed the world situation all these fifty-six years not because of my personal interest but for the Lord's interests.

From our youth we studied not only the Bible but also the history of the church and the biographies and writings of the spiritual seekers of the past. Then we came to realize that we also needed to know the world situation. Otherwise we would still be partially in darkness. Most of the other co-workers and myself, under the leading of Brother Watchman Nee, studied these matters. He read books which I did not read, yet he conversed with me on many occasions about the facts of church history. We knew the writings of the Church Fathers and the great teachers who came later. Doctrinally and theologically, we learned what went on from the time of the Apostle Paul down to the present age.

AN EXTRAORDINARY COUNTRY

It is clear that the Soviet Union is facing serious problems today, while the United States is trying to keep peace for the whole world. In the world today, what country is taking the lead? Who keeps the order and maintains the peace? What country is the geographic center? Who is on top financially, industrially, educationally, and culturally? It is the United States. Who brought this about? God did it. This is altogether God's doing. As lovers of God and seekers of the Lord, and as those in the recovery, we worship the Lord for such a country.

This is not to say that the United States has no sin. Just look at the sinfulness in the one city of San Francisco, not to mention Chicago, New York, Los Angeles, and Las Vegas. I do not mean that the United States is pure or moral. What I mean is that there is no other country where there is such freedom of speech. I believe this freedom has been arranged by God for us to be here to release the truth without restriction or fear. No other country is like it.

The United States is extraordinary. Its people have the highest education and culture. Because of this, they can understand what I am saying. If I were speaking to a primitive, backward people, I doubt that they would be able to apprehend what I was saying. Here it is easy. We have the freedom and boldness to utter whatever the Lord has shown us.

I thank the Lord that He preserved this continent for fifty-five hundred years. Then He sent cultured, godly people to found this nation. Now it is the leading country. All this is the Lord's sovereignty.

THE SEVEN STAGES OF MANKIND'S HISTORY

From the spiritual heavenly point of view, human history has seven stages, with the present stage being the last, that is, before the millennium. The first is the primitive stage, from Adam to Abraham. The second is the formation of the kingdom of Israel as God's kingdom on earth. This stage lasted from Abraham to Solomon. The third stage is the desolation of the kingdom of Israel. The kingdoms of Babylon, Media-Persia, and Greece under Alexander the Great desolated Israel. This was God's judgment on His degraded people.

The fourth stage is the Roman Empire. It also desolated Israel to some extent, but not as much as the others, at least, not until A.D. 70, when Titus destroyed Jerusalem. Josephus describes how terrible that destruction was. The Roman Empire was prepared and used by God for the accomplishment of redemption and for the spread of the good news around the Mediterranean Sea. In the centuries which followed, however, the Roman Empire brought in the Roman Church, which ruined the gospel and ushered in ten centuries of the Dark Ages.

The fifth stage is the Reformation. It extends from the time of Martin Luther down to the last century. During this stage many new things came in that changed human history. There was the discovery and settlement of the new land. There was the reformation of the so-called Christian Church. Germany was the power used by God during this stage.

The sixth stage is the furtherance of the gospel preaching and the Word of God. This was accomplished by God under the power of Great Britain. Spain was defeated and Britain was used to maintain order on the earth so that the gospel could be preached worldwide and the truth brought to every corner of the globe. Now the Bible has been translated at least in part into most languages. So the Word of God has been spreading to every part of the earth, like the gospel. This is the Lord's doing.

Is this all? Is this sixth stage the final one? If so, what does the Lord gain? The central vision of the Apostle Paul's completing ministry has not been adequately touched, nor has the mending ministry of John. Few Christian teachers even know the term, the mending ministry. The inner-life people know a little of Paul's completing ministry, but what they have touched mainly concerns Christ, His death, and the resurrection. They have not seen much concerning the all-inclusive and all-extensive Christ in Philippians and Colossians. They have little to say of the Body of Christ. As for John's mending ministry, what is ministered is mostly in a superficial way. Many do not know in a clear way what regeneration is. Today we are in the seventh or final stage, when the Lord would recover the completing ministry of Paul and the mending ministry of John.

THE NEED FOR THE FINAL STAGE

Furthermore, we need to realize at least five main aspects concerning the church. First of all, it is a gathering or assembly of the saints. In the last century the Brethren saw this and gave up the denominations, organizations, chapels, and cathedrals to come back to the Bible to meet in the name of the Lord Jesus. They have recovered the aspect of the church as an assembly. This, however, is still too shallow.

The church is also the Body of Christ, the new man, the lampstand, and the bride. Not many teachers have touched these four aspects adequately. Until these four aspects of the church are realized, both Paul's completing ministry and

John's mending ministry cannot be fulfilled; thus, the Lord has still not accomplished His purpose and has no way to come back.

God's purpose is not completed by gospel preaching, Bible teaching, and scriptural meetings alone. Without the nineteen books of Paul and John, there is no completion. Although Christians today have these nineteen books, they don't pay much attention to these two ministries.

Many may refer to Paul's books, but few stress the completing ministry. What is Paul's completing ministry? It is the mystery of God, which is Christ, and the mystery of Christ, which is the church. Most Bible readers have studied Paul's Epistles and have seen these terms (Col. 2:2; Eph. 3:4), but they probably do not have much understanding of what they mean.

John's mending ministry presents the church as a lampstand (Rev. 1:11-12). Christians today speak little concerning this aspect of the church. The lampstand portrays the church as the embodiment of the Triune God. Its golden nature signifies the Father as the source. Its shape signifies the Son as the embodiment of the Father. The seven lamps shining speak of the seven Spirits as the expression of the Triune God. The church as the lampstand, then, is the Triune God embodied and expressed in His redeemed people.

We have given many messages concerning these two ministries of Paul and John. As we have studied Galatians, Ephesians, Philippians, and Colossians, what an all-inclusive and all-extensive Christ we have seen as the mystery of God! Many messages have been given on the church as the Body of Christ, the new man, the lampstand, and the bride.

Since 1969 by His mercy we have had many messages on the book of Revelation. We have had a thorough study of this book in every aspect. We have especially emphasized the seven Spirits, the lampstand, the testimony of Jesus, the eating of the tree of life, the building up of pillars in the temple of God, the promise of partaking of the tree of life, and the call to drink of the living water. As you can see from the notes in the Recovery Version, we have not neglected the ten horns and the other matters of prophecy either, although we did concentrate on the life side, the spiritual side.

THE FINALITY OF THE WORLD SITUATION

Just a few days ago I came across an old book by A. T. Pierson. At the end of the last century he visited Philadelphia and, while there, gave a series of messages which he called *The New Acts of the Apostles*. This is a good title, reminding us that the book of Acts does not really have only twenty-eight chapters. We are still in the continuation of Acts; by our time perhaps there are two hundred eighty chapters!

In this book Pierson says that God kept a continent veiled for five thousand years, rending the veil only when a reformed church with an unchained Bible was ready to enter it. This thought is quite similar to what we have pointed out in these messages. But he adds, "and make it the theater of new gospel triumphs." Our view differs from his in this. I do not believe that America was preserved only for new triumphs in gospel preaching. Those who came to the new continent already had access to the gospel. I believe this country was raised up by the Lord for the recovery. The status of the United States as the world's leading nation is the world's ultimate situation for the Lord's ultimate recovery.

If the Bible has been nearly fully recovered, what about the present world situation? Do you believe that God will raise up yet another power after the United States? All the previous world powers were replaced. Babylon was overcome by Media-Persia. Greece followed Media-Persia as the leading world power. Then came the Roman Empire. Then the European nations gradually arose, with Germany, Spain, and Great Britain at different times being foremost. Now that the United States has come into the lead, it seems clear from the present world situation that it will not be replaced.

At the war of Armageddon there will be three military powers gathered. One will be from the west, Europe, under Antichrist. One will be from the north, Russia. The third will be from the sunrise. There is no hint of what the position of the United States will be. Do not think that Antichrist with his restored Roman Empire will replace the United States.

This country, symbolized by an eagle, is bordered by two oceans which separate it from other lands. In Daniel a ram symbolizes Media-Persia (Dan. 8:20), and a goat represents Greece (v. 21). As G. H. Pember relates, these are the ancient symbols of those countries. The ram has been found engraved on ancient Persian coins and sculptures. The goat is depicted on old coins from Macedonia; the waters to the east of it were called the Aegean, meaning Goat Sea.

Today there are a number of small countries around the Mediterranean Sea, besides the other countries in Europe. It may be that the peoples in these small, independent nations would like to have a strong leader unite them and thus rescue them from their weak position. Antichrist may take the chance to rise up and unite these countries, thus restoring the old Roman Empire. But this new empire will not replace the United States nor will it defeat Russia. It will also not defeat the two hundred million horsemen from the sunrise (Rev. 9:16). Since Antichrist with his restored Roman Empire will not defeat Russia, nor the east, neither will he be able to replace the United States. Thus there will be four sources of power. Three will go to Armageddon in order to get the wealth there. Probably the wealth will come from the oil.

THE NEED FOR A VISION

Under God's sovereignty the gospel has been preached to every corner of the earth. The Bible prophesied this would happen, and it has. The Bible has been taught in every country. And God did gain some proper meetings even a hundred fifty years ago. Even though God has gained this much, however, He has never gained the central line of His purpose, that is, Christ as the mystery of God and the church as the mystery of Christ. This church as the mystery of Christ must be the Body, not just the assembly. It must be the new man. It must be the lampstand. It must be the bride.

What is our responsibility? We must look to the Lord to show us the central vision of Paul's completing ministry and of John's mending ministry. What is the vision? It is the all-inclusive, extensive, subjective Christ, who is the life-giving Spirit as the consummate expression of the Triune God now that He has accomplished all the processes. We must see Christ as such a One. We must live such a Christ. He must be our life. He must be our living. He must be our daily family life. He must be our church life.

We have the example of Paul. When he went to the cultured Greek city of Corinth, he determined not to go with excellence of speech. Just because of its high culture, he would not use eloquent words of wisdom. "For I determined not to know anything among you except Jesus Christ, and this One crucified" (1 Cor. 2:1-4). His word to the Corinthians was that they as believers were joined to the Lord as one spirit (6:17). To the Philippians he said, "To me to live is Christ" (Phil. 1:21). It was his expectation and hope that Christ would be magnified in his body "whether through life or through death" (v. 20).

I am afraid what you may be impressed with is gospel preaching, Bible teaching, and good meetings. You may not have much realization of this all-inclusive Christ. Our responsibility is to live this Christ, to bring this Christ wherever we go. To do this requires that we be fully in the spirit, that we live by the Spirit, and that we walk by the Spirit, even by the sevenfold intensified Spirit.

Those who live Christ, who live in the spirit, are the actual Body of Christ corporately. This Body is one (Eph. 4:4). They are also the new man in actuality, a new creation with a new living to express the Triune God.

OUR RESPONSIBILITY

What is our burden? What is our responsibility? We must not just preach the gospel. We must bear the testimony of Jesus, as Revelation says (1:2, 9). We must be witnesses to Him, as Acts 1:8 tells us. We must bring forth fruit by abiding in Him, as John 15:5 and 16 tell us. This is the proper preaching of the gospel. There is no need to use any gimmicks. We must lay our gimmicks aside, just as Paul determined not to use excellence of speech. Our responsibility is to live Christ, to bear a living witness to Him in our daily life, to know nothing but Christ, the all-inclusive One revealed in the completing ministry of Paul and the mending ministry of John.

Then, whenever we come together, we are one Body and the one new man. There is no discrimination, whatever our background is. Praise the Lord for such a country as the United States! The other countries are made up of people of one nationality. Germany, for example, is composed of Germans. The United States is the only country that comprises all different races and national backgrounds; that is why it is called a melting pot. Is it not sovereign of the Lord that there should be such a nation right in the center of the inhabited earth? How good for the new man! Here there cannot be Greek or Jew, black or white, Oriental or Westerner, "but Christ is all and in all" (Col. 3:11).

Our ultimate responsibility is to live Christ and to meet together in our locality in such a way that we may be the Body, the new man, the lampstand, and the bride. We meet in oneness. The Christ we live and preach is not divided. The Christ we testify is not divided. We live Him according to this view we have of Him. We live the all-inclusive, extensive Christ who is now the life-giving Spirit as the ultimate expression of the Triune God after many processes. And we meet together according to locality as the church, the church which is not only an assembly but also the Body, the new man, the lampstand, and the bride. We also practice the genuine oneness in every locality—one Body, one Spirit, one city, one church. Such a living is our ultimate responsibility.

By Twos to Different Countries

The spreading of the Lord's recovery must be considered part of our ultimate responsibility. When the Lord was on earth, He sent the disciples out two by two. When the church testimony was spreading, Paul and Barnabas also went out by two. I believe this is a divine principle. Suppose some are burdened to go to other countries. How will they make a living? It will be hard in a new country. I believe, however, that the rest who remain here could pick up the burden to support them.

Those who go out by twos to foreign countries may mostly go to study, to attend school, to learn the language. They can also contact people. Foreign students find it easy to contact other students and teachers. Out of these contacts they will be able to pass on Jesus Christ. There will be no need to be concerned about living expenses, because the saints here will support them. This will be easy to carry out, and it is the biblical way.

Small Lampstands Raised Up

After a few years there could be a small testimony in many countries. The two in each place, as they are studying, or working, or just contacting people, could bring at least ten to the Lord. Then there would be twelve meeting together as a small lampstand. A lampstand is not big like a lighthouse; I believe the Bible uses the lampstand to signify the church to give the sense that the church does not have to be a big thing.

Suppose two brothers go with their wives to Athens, Greece. With four of them there, all studying and contacting other students, do you not believe that they can bring in at least ten within five years? Then there can be fourteen meeting there as the church in Athens! They will go there not like traditional missionaries but rather as the high-class witnesses to Jesus Christ. They will bring the high gospel to Athens. They will bring the deeper knowledge of the Bible. They will bring Christ. They will bring the testimony of Jesus, that is, the Body, the new man, the lampstand, and the bride.

A Sober Consideration Needed

I believe this may be the Lord's way to prepare His bride (Rev. 19:7-8). Now that I have spoken to you, I have fulfilled my responsibility. Now the responsibility is yours. As you consider what you have read in these chapters of the world situation and of the Lord's recovery, what will you do? Will you simply stay where you are and make a good living? Will you be content with good meetings? Good meetings are enjoyable, yet would the Lord not lead you out? Be sober and alert that the Lord may grant you the proper guidance—whether to stay or to go, where to go, and the way to go. If He leads you to stay, how much responsibility should you bear for those who go out in His name for His recovery by faith to other countries? A move like this is living; it is the Lord's move in His Body.

This is the ultimate responsibility we must bear for the Lord's ultimate recovery under the present ultimate world situation. We thank Him for this situation. We thank Him for the recovery. We thank Him for His grace, which will enable us to bear such a responsibility.

ABOUT THE AUTHOR

Witness Lee was born in 1905 in northern China and raised in a Christian family. At age 19 he was fully captured for Christ and immediately consecrated himself to preach the gospel for the rest of his life. Early in his service, he met Watchman Nee, a renowned preacher, teacher, and writer. Witness Lee labored together with Watchman Nee under his direction. In 1934 Watchman Nee entrusted Witness Lee with the responsibility for his publication operation, called the Shanghai Gospel Bookroom.

Prior to the Communist takeover in 1949, Witness Lee was sent by Watchman Nee and his other co-workers to Taiwan to ensure that the things delivered to them by the Lord would not be lost. Watchman Nee instructed Witness Lee to continue the former's publishing operation abroad as the Taiwan Gospel Bookroom, which has been publicly recognized as the publisher of Watchman Nee's works outside China. Witness Lee's work in Taiwan manifested the Lord's abundant blessing. From a mere 350 believers, newly fled from the mainland, the churches in Taiwan grew to 20,000 in five years.

In 1962 Witness Lee felt led of the Lord to come to the United States, and he began to minister in Los Angeles. During his 35 years of service in the U.S., he ministered in weekly meetings and weekend conferences, delivering several thousand spoken messages. Much of his speaking has since been published as over 400 titles. Many of these have been translated into over fourteen languages. He gave his last public conference in February 1997 at the age of 91.

He leaves behind a prolific presentation of the truth in the Bible. His major work, *Life-study of the Bible,* comprises over 25,000 pages of commentary on every book of the Bible from the perspective of the believers' enjoyment and experience of God's divine life in Christ through the Holy Spirit. Witness Lee was the chief editor of a new translation of the New Testament into Chinese called the Recovery Version and directed the translation of the same into English. The Recovery Version also appears in a number of other languages. He provided an extensive body of footnotes, outlines, and spiritual cross references. A radio broadcast of his messages can be heard on Christian radio stations in the United States. In 1965 Witness Lee founded Living Stream Ministry, a non-profit corporation, located in Anaheim, California, which officially presents his and Watchman Nee's ministry.

Witness Lee's ministry emphasizes the experience of Christ as life and the practical oneness of the believers as the Body of Christ. Stressing the importance of attending to both these matters, he led the churches under his care to grow in Christian life and function. He was unbending in his conviction that God's goal is not narrow sectarianism but the Body of Christ. In time, believers began to meet simply as the church in their localities in response to this conviction. In recent years a number of new churches have been raised up in Russia and in many European countries.

OTHER BOOKS PUBLISHED BY
Living Stream Ministry

Titles by Witness Lee:

Titles by Watchman Nee:

Available at
Christian bookstores, or contact Living Stream Ministry
2431 W. La Palma Ave. • Anaheim, CA 92801
1-800-549-5164 • www.livingstream.com